OVERWHELMING
~ MINORITY ~

By J. Ted Esler

Some do great things in

the pursuit of adventure,

others have adventure

while pursuing great things.

BottomLine

Published by BottomLine Media
ISBN: 0-9759997-1-9
Copyright © 2006 The unauthorized reproduction of this
material is encouraged.
Printed in Bloomingdale, Illinois by Envision Graphics
Edited by Caryn M. Pederson and Lorie Munizzi
Cover and Page Design by Flory Design

∼ TABLE *of* CONTENTS ∼

This book is dedicated to my wife, Annette. She leapt across a chasm of faith and took her small children into a war zone, trusting that God would not only keep us safe, but enable us to thrive. She made this this story possible.

~ACKNOWLEDGEMENTS~

I remember first telling my dad that I would be leaving my computer consulting job to work as a missionary. "How much do they pay?" he asked, only to learn that I would have to find my own means of support to do this job. After his initial surprise, he responded, "If that's what you want to do, then you should do it." Thanks, Dad, I know it wasn't easy saying goodbye to the grandchildren. My mom prayed for me during the darkest, most rebellious days of my life right into the most wonderful, Spirit-filled times. Thanks, Mom; you've been the hand that rocks the cradle.

Hundreds are a part of this story. So many gave financially, so many prayed, and so many visited. Thanks Grace Church Roseville (Roseville, Minnesota)—and countless other churches—for standing with us. The world's missionary work rests on the shoulders of gathering communities like these. There are also many individual donors and prayer warriors who loved us through the years.

PIONEERS is a unique movement that strives to make the most of each person's God-given vision. The leadership of PIONEERS "gets it" when it comes to balancing individual direction with a team vision. Thanks to PIONEERS for making this book possible. Thanks to Bob Hitching, who helped me to get started, and to Caryn Pederson, who helped me to finish.

Our family motto is "Blessed to be a Blessing." Caleb, Joshua, David, Abigail, and Sarah were with Annette and I through every step of the journey recorded in this small book. They were the bright faces, smiles, and hugs that lifted our souls and gave us joy. What blessings you've been!

—— ❦ ——

This book covers a relatively brief time in the history of the church in Bosnia and Herzegovina, but I believe it is an important time. I was greatly blessed to appear on the scene for a few short years and play a small role in what is an epic struggle on the Balkan Peninsula. From 1992 to 2000, the Bosnian church exploded from a few small embattled congregations to 500-600 people spread across a number of small but growing fellowships. If one were to compile a history of the evangelical church in Bosnia there would be no doubt that these years would be considered the time of greatest expansion.

I am writing this down not to suggest what our family experienced and did was of some great historical consequence. In fact, one of the lessons I learned was quite the opposite: God is writing history, not us. Rather, I hope to convey the truth that a small group of people can make a difference—eternally.

In 2005, the Irish Republican Army (IRA) stated that they would voluntarily begin a ceasefire. The ensuing news coverage revealed that the IRA consisted of approximately 200-300 soldiers. It was a revelation that shocked many; how could such a small group of people keep the British Army at bay for so long? Terrorism is similar. Small groups can yield incredible influence.

This story is about my family's sojourn to Bosnia and what happened after we arrived. It reveals a small sliver of the people and experiences through which God blessed us. Not every stone is turned over, nor is each person's role described and defined. Some have expressly asked not to be named. For that reason, we have changed the names of all of the people in the book who are Bosnian.

Before the Turkish Muslims took over the southern half of the Balkan Peninsula, there was a group of people in Bosnia and Herzegovina called the Bogomils. Only a few facts are known about these people. They resolutely maintained their independence from the Orthodox and Catholic churches. Many attribute their faith to a 13th century mystic, yet few really know the details of this leader or his belief system. They left large gravestones scattered across Bosnia with very peculiar engravings. It is believed that they practiced a simple form of Christianity and that their priests were encouraged to marry.

We will never really know, of course, what these people believed, but there is scholarship which suggests that they were similar to Protestants that would appear in the coming centuries. If so, they were squeezed out when the Muslims entered Central Bosnia. Perhaps they joined with the Catholic or Orthodox believers. All we know is that they somehow dissipated and left little behind.

The Bosnian War of the late 20th century will most likely not be the last to descend on this war-weary land. If, however, the fighting begins anew, I am confident that its evangelical minority will not simply dissipate like the Bogomils. Their roots, though small, have already begun to wind their way tenaciously through the rocky soil of the Bosnian Mountains.

CHAPTER 1

A FAMILY GOES TO WAR

—▪—

"A great door of opportunity has opened for me
but there are many adversaries."
—THE APOSTLE PAUL, 1 CORINTHIANS 1:9

Two men pass a tiny newspaper clipping across the table in the Belgrade café, Zlatna Moruna. Under the light of a gas lamp, conspirators against the European political order decipher coded words and understand that Archduke Franz Ferdinand would be in Sarajevo. He was coming to oversee military maneuvers taking place in the neighboring mountains. At this small table in an obscure little café, a plot is born that would transform the world.

A small band of conspirators later organize to line the streets of Sarajevo. A botched attempt to throw a grenade at the archduke results in a hasty meeting in the Town Hall. It is prudently decided that the archduke and his wife should leave the city at once. They climb aboard their open motorcar and begin the speedy journey out of the city. As they near the Miljacka River, they slow to make a turn. Gavrillo Princip, nervous but determined, stands waiting in the shadows. Princip suffers from tuberculosis and knows that his life will end soon enough. This fact combined with his desire for Bosnian independence drives him to a final, desperate end. Stepping from his hiding place, he withdraws a pistol from his coat and fires two shots. The first hits Sophie, the Archduke's wife. An expecting mother, she dies instantly. The second bullet finds its target. Ferdinand's last words are but one: "Sophie." His head falls back and he collapses.

Within weeks the entire political structure of Europe also collapses. Nations bound by treaty join in war against others in an interlocking set of unforeseen consequences. Blood fills the trenches of Europe for the next five years, and we call it World War I.

Nobody imagined that this small minority could so change the face of the world.

Eighty years later, my family settled in for the night in our rented home, just miles from the historic spot where Gavrillo changed the world. Our second-story bedroom felt like a cellar. Many of the windows were smashed out, the windows replaced with plywood and plastic. Shrapnel pockmarks in the walls gave the house a feeling of insecurity. The electricity was off and candles caused shadows to dance across the walls like a silhouette puppet show. I glanced across the room at my wife, Annette, who was beginning to drift off to sleep. She looked so wholesome and gentle in a place that had seen such evil and suffering. The children were asleep on the floor since we had just moved into the house and had not yet located beds. Wrapped in sleeping bags, their little bodies seemed so innocent, so different from everything around us.

"Only a fool would take his family into Bosnia at a time like this." The remarks of friends at home hung in my mind, declaring the majority view of my own culture that honors safety almost above everything. Theologians teach that the safest place on earth is in the center of God's will. That is easy to say, but quite another to actually live out. And when lived, it is harder still to experience in the midst of a struggle.

Suddenly, a whole series of explosions coming from

the direction of the NATO army base interrupted my thoughts. Next door, screaming immediately followed. Our little neighbor Tanya could be heard crying and others called out in panic. They knew this meant more bombs, more killing, more angst, and more fear. Then the machine guns started their rata-tat-tat sounds from the streets. The children awoke and huddled together; the sounds of crying from the flat below us punctuated the atmosphere with a strange sense of foreboding. I crept slowly across the room toward the door that led to the balcony, wondering about the will of God and all the pious theory that I had learned and claimed as my own regarding sovereignty and divine protection.

The sky was full of color and sound. Then, in one of those moments tinged with both comedy and tragedy, I realized what was happening. The American forces at the NATO base were having their Fourth of July fireworks celebration. The noise agitated the Bosnians in the city, and they were firing their guns into the air. I stood on the balcony and called for Annette and the kids to come out and enjoy the show even while our neighbors were still running toward their cellars.

The noise agitated the Bosnians in the city, and they were firing their guns into the air.

Looking out across the sky I wondered about my cultural sensitivity. I vowed to learn a lesson from this as I sought to bring the gospel into this culture. It had not known much sensitivity through the centuries.

The children went back to sleep and the sounds of fear from the family next door slowly dissipated into the night. Annette and I stood on the balcony and looked out into the city. Together we held hands, as much for comfort as for romance, and prayed that God would build his church and the gates of hell, so very present, would not prevail against her. We were foolish enough to believe it.

Naive would only begin to describe our decision to move to a country torn asunder, which is what shattered, mine-ridden Bosnia was like in 1996. I was a computer consultant in 1988 when Annette and I first began to consider overseas service with a Christian organization. As a "contract programmer" I was making pretty good money for a 26-year-old. My father was astounded at the thought of somebody making an hourly wage that equaled a full day's pay for some of the young men who worked for him in his drywall business. I spent one summer on a paint crew that worked for my dad. That was all it took for me to re-align my liberal arts major to something a bit more practical and lucrative than "Speech Communication."

As we investigated our options, our church asked us to get some training in cross-cultural ministry. Our church had a relationship with a missionary training school in Belize, Central America, and we concluded that God was calling us to consider some sort of work in a tribal area. We saw the pictures of bone-nosed Papua New Guineans and decided that this was for us. Apparently, God had other plans.

Our first stop would be an old hotel in Kissimmee, Florida, that was converted into a training school. After a few months in the classroom studying linguistics and cultural anthropology, we would then have the opportunity to live in a Mayan village in order to practice what we learned.

Going to the training program was probably the hardest transition that I have ever made. One week I was a computer consultant in corporate America, enjoying all the perks that business in the high-tech sector had to offer. The next week our entire family was living in an old hotel room. There was no kitchen, except for an electric fry pan and microwave. We washed baby bottoms and dinner dishes in the bathtub.

I felt a loss of identity. I hadn't realized how much pride I tied into my role as a computer entrepreneur. Having been stripped of all that, all I had left was the title "missionary." This is not exactly a highly esteemed role in the eyes of the world.

High mountains and low valleys characterized our time in Belize. It was like a camping trip that never ended. One evening during our first few weeks there, I heard leaves rustling. I shined the flashlight up in the trees, to find monkeys looking down—curious what I was doing in their jungle. I was excited about being in this place that was as foreign as possible to all I had known. But it was an excitement that wouldn't last long.

Our two boys loved living there. We lived so close to the Mayans that we shared a wall with the adjacent house and all their children would play with ours. One could almost say that we shared kids as well as the wall. The Mayans are dark, with jet-black hair and beautiful brown eyes—quite a contrast to Joshua's fair skin and white hair! As he walked through the village they would come up to him just to touch that hair. Wherever we went we could hear the children whispering to one another, "Joshua, Joshua, Joshua" and calling him an angel.

Each day we would learn a phrase or two that we would then take on "language rounds" in which we would walk from house to house practicing our roughly formed syllables. We kept logbooks of cultural observations. We noted how the economic and political structure of the village worked. While the modernizing world was certainly impacting this far away place, old traditions, animism, and witchcraft continued to hold power over many of these people.

After spending a few months in Belize, learning how to study a language and culture, we made our way back to Minneapolis and waited for the recommendations from the training school to be given to our church. The report was not as positive as we had hoped. It is hard to explain the feelings of confusion I had when I read that although we were encouraged to pursue overseas ministry, it was a qualified recommendation. After walking away from my career, selling the house, and seeing Annette suffer through numerous trials it didn't seem quite fair. We began to conclude that perhaps missionary work was not for us.

I was still close enough to the computer scene to brush up and get back into the world of consulting. I felt both a sense of relief and entrapment at the thought of not being able to be a missionary. I was confused and cried out to God for direction.

During that period of much soul searching and tender-hearted prayers, I called our mission agency to let them know what we were thinking. Before going to Belize we joined Pioneers. We chose this agency for two reasons. First, they start new churches among unreached people groups. There are many great agencies out there doing many things for the kingdom of God. There are few, however, that are focused primarily on unreached people groups and fewer still that see church planting as the top priority. The second reason is that when I called them, they were genuinely interested in our plans. They treated us like real people. So, in light of the confusion I was now feeling, I flew out to see the leadership and discuss the future with them.

Meeting then President John Fletcher and Chairman of the Board Bob Hitching, we discussed my family's experience in Belize. Looking at the needs among the unreached and evaluating our training experience, I knew that God was pressing us to move forward and not give up on our desire to serve cross-culturally.

At the same time, it was more than apparent that the jungle was not for us. We decided to cast our nets toward unreached peoples living in urban centers. So, in 1990 we began praying for the Muslims of Sarajevo, Yugoslavia. With counsel from our church, we prepared to move to Eastern Europe. Little did we know that within a year and a half the Balkan Peninsula would be enveloped in a war that would lay siege to our new home.

Our task was simple enough. Like Gavrillo Princip and his rebel band, we were to come together with like-minded conspirators and, with limited resources and personnel, become an overwhelming minority. Only this time we wouldn't be shooting bullets in an effort to stir up hatred and dissension. We were to communicate forgiveness and reconciliation as can only be found in the name of Christ. I was about to learn how difficult that would be.

CHAPTER 2

NAIVE

—◆—

"Toto, we're not in Kansas anymore."
—DOROTHY, *THE WIZARD OF OZ*

The Serbian Army seized about one-third of Croatian territory when Croatia declared independence from Yugoslavia in 1991. Of course, the Serbs had lived in this land for centuries and didn't particularly see it as "seizing" anything. This region was called "The Krajina" and was initially settled by the Serbs to create a buffer zone between the Hapsburgs and the Turks. History was hard on the Krajina Serbs, and trust was not on the side of the Croatians when they voted for succession.

Croatia was almost cut in two in a pincerlike move by the Serbian forces and it looked pretty bleak for Croatia. In the spring of 1992 they cried "Uncle" and asked for help. The United Nations was called in to put an end to hostilities. The day they moved was the first day I set foot in Croatia, making a trip in preparation for our family's arrival.

Since living in Sarajevo with a family was impossible for the foreseeable future, Croatia became our home. This country is one of Eastern Europe's most beautiful places. The crystal blue waters of the island-studded coast give way to the Velebit Mountains that rise up in jagged defiance of the sea's flat surface. There are plains, forests, rivers, and cities, all pocked with reminders of a time less complex. Croatia is a country that drips with medieval heritage. The European caricature of feudal kingdoms comes alive looking at the castles and outposts of the Hapsburg Empire.

We enrolled in language school and began the laborious process of preparing to minister in Serbo-Croatian (now identified by its three major dialects: Bosnia, Croatian, and Serbian). Our time in Croatia was initially intended to be a step on the path to Sarajevo, but we soon began to think we were destined to stay put. In retrospect this delay was a great blessing because we were able to concentrate so fully on language studies.

The beginnings of what would become this overwhelming minority began to take shape as other team members arrived to begin their studies as well. The war in Bosnia had a positive effect on the initial team members: we could do little but study language. It was too dangerous to contemplate a move into Bosnia with little ones. Our son David was just a baby when we arrived. Our daughter Sarah came the next summer, and our family was now six!

We entered Croatia soon after they had claimed their independence from Yugoslavia. During the communist era it was forbidden to show any signs of Croatian nationalism. The checkerboard symbol—that means as much to Croatians as Old Glory does to Americans—was forbidden under the communists. Now, one could not escape the pervasive presence of Croatian patriotic fervor most often in the form of that very checkerboard symbol.

Ban Jelacic was a Croatian king and national hero. His statue once stood over the main square but was removed during the years of socialism. A story is told about a man who obtained the disgraced statue and cut it up into chunks so that it could be buried in the floor of his garage. When the day came for Croatia to once again be Croatian, the statue was dug up and put back together. In an incredible ceremony that took place before thousands of people live and millions via television, a helicopter brought the statue back to its original place on "Ban Jelacic Square." It was a time of hope and promise for Croatia. It was history in the making, and we had front-row seats to all that was happening. Little did we realize how much history we would witness in these emerging nations.

The physical damage of war is mild compared to the broken hearts and ruined lives. One evening I met a Croatian man who had suffered deeply, and his story shocked the foundations of my faith.

As we sat down over cups of Turkish coffee he eventually learned that we were there as missionaries. He asked what a missionary did because he had never met one before. I told him that missionaries share the love of God. They are there to talk about forgiveness because Christ came to forgive the world. Somewhere in the course of the conversation I made the glib comment that in Christ we can learn to forgive anybody for anything.

"Really?" he asked, leaning forward with a blaze in his eyes. He began to tell me about his family and how they died. During the initial days of the war some villages were taken and lost by either side, changing hands in the course of a couple days. This man was from such a village. The Serbs came in and took the whole community. He himself had already been called to be a soldier and was away in training when the attack came. When news reached him that his village was under attack, he was released to go back. He fought for a couple of days and the Croatians took the village from the Serbs. As soon as the village was secured, the commander said, "You can go check on your homes." As he walked up the road to his home, he feared the worst, but nothing could prepare him for what he saw.

The Serbian symbol was painted on the outside of his home in red spray paint. He opened door of his house slowly as he cautiously looked for landmines. He walked into the first room and found his wife on the table. Her arms had been tied down and her legs spread out, lying naked from the waist down. She was brutally raped. Her throat had been cut and black dried blood was everywhere. He was shocked and began to vomit. The door creaked shut behind him, and as he turned around he saw his little girl nailed to the door by her hands and her wrists, elbows and feet in a crucifix position.

He...asked in a low whisper: "Are you telling me that I can forgive that?"

As he told the story, he paused while I stared at the floor. He reached out and grabbed my arm, and pulled me within inches of his face and asked in a low whisper: "Are you telling me that I can forgive that? It can't be forgiven and it should not be forgiven!" He released his grip on me. I was shaken as he got up and left the room.

If that was Annette on the table and our youngest, Abigail, nailed to the door, could I forgive? I don't know. How could I share the simple message of Christ in a place like this, where simplicity was complicated by humanity's dark hatred?

— ❧ —

CHAPTER 3

BLOWN AWAY

——

"The Lord's mercy often rides to the door of our heart upon the black horse of affliction." —CHARLES H. SPURGEON

Could we safely move into Sarajevo, the most hotly contested real estate on the planet? Other team members and their families had moved into other parts of Bosnia in 1995, and a church was born in the central Bosnian city of Novi Travnik.

Annette, Abigail (just 3½ weeks old), and I drove from Zagreb to Novi Travnik, where a teammate, Rob, joined us. Our route to Sarajevo in 1996 took us over the bridges built by NATO and along the roads that were once a part of the Roman Empire's wild frontier.

Damage was evident all the way from southern Croatia on the south, but the magnitude of damage done to Sarajevo made the rest of the conflict seem insignificant.

More than 1 million mortars fell on the city during its more than 3½ years under siege. The enormity of the damage bowled us over and struck us deeply. A light post wasn't simply scarred by a bullet hole; 20 or 30 shrapnel holes marked a light post from top to bottom. The roads were splattered with the marks of exploding mortars.

The garbage piled up after years of no garbage collection. People, afraid to leave their apartments for fear of snipers, had no choice but to toss it out their windows. There was garbage everywhere, and it was being gathered into large piles for burning. This produced a peculiar, acrid smoke that hung over the whole city and caused a gray haze. Fires constantly burned and smoldered throughout the city, illuminating the shiny barbed wire barricades scattered here and there.

There were wrecked cars everywhere. No street was without a pile of mangled automobile wreckage. On the main road that goes all the way through Sarajevo (dubbed Sniper Alley) driving was a free for all. There were no lines on the road to tell one lane from the next. No street lights were in operation, and each intersection became a game of chicken as drivers made their way through town at whatever speed the driver deemed appropriate.

During the siege, cars would madly dash through

the city without lights in order to evade ammunition. U.N. vehicles would move wreckage off to one side the next day. More people died on Sniper Alley as a result of traffic accidents than bullets.

Some roads sported "Sniper Covers." Snipers, safely hidden in high-rise apartment building windows, often sighted their rifles to peer down the length of the main streets. In order to obscure their deadly view, Sarajevans hung cables across the street between buildings. They then hung large Turkish rugs on the cables. This kept snipers from being able to see their hapless targets carrying water, wood, and other supplies. When we arrived, a number of the main intersections still had these "sniper covers" stretched out across them.

Mosques, a favorite target of Serb mortars, silently told of the war. Once-proud minarets only stood half their size. The damaged columns were soon repaired by Saudi Arabian donations, and topped with shiny new copper tops and speakers ready to blare out the call to prayer.

Helicopters paroled the perimeters of the mountaintops with their chopping blades. Diesel-powered armored vehicles revved up and down the winding roads leading to and from the valley. Each had a grim-faced NATO soldier in the machine-gun turret.

Some of the buildings had no outside walls whatso-
ever, just the cement dividers between the floors and inside walls jutting out into open space. A high-rise building of 20 or 30 floors was skinned from top to bottom
allowing a view of each apartment. People inhabited
many of these apartments, having strung white plastic
sheets bearing the blue United Nations insignia over the
openings.

For our first night in Sarajevo we rented a room from
Ramiza, a middle-aged Bosnian woman who lived in a
high-rise apartment complex. Our teammate, Rob, had
met her through a common friend in another city, Zenica.
She rented her only two bedrooms to us and agreed to fix
meals for us. Rob had to pay her half the rent money up-
front so that she could buy groceries in order to feed us.
When I went to use the restroom, I found small pieces of
paper that were cut up for use as toilet paper—she could
not afford to purchase tissues.

During the war, Ramiza's apartment complex was
in the line of fire. One of a number of towering buildings along the main road running through Sarajevo,
the early days of the war offered an anxious view of the
fighting that ensued below. Soon, however, the enemy
was firing from building to building as Serbian residents
took sides with their comrades firing into the city. Anti-

sniper teams were organized, sitting for long hours in the dark until a muzzle flash was detected in the windows of a neighboring building. Counting floors and windows they determined which apartment held the enemy and they attacked from inside. Terrified residents laid flat on their beds as mortar shells were hand-tossed into these small apartments to deadly effect.

A gas pipe was installed in Ramiza's apartment. There was no regulating device on it other than a simple switch to turn the flow of gas on or off. The gas ran out the end of a metal element and was lit. This simple but extremely dangerous heating source was a great improvement over the previous months. By the end of the siege Ramiza sold all that she had for either fuel or food. Her furniture partially deconstructed in order to use larger pieces of wood for the fire. She recounted that a pair of jeans, rolled tightly and bound with wire, could burn through the night keeping a family alive in the ice-cold mountain winter. A small package of coffee cost about $50. Cigarettes were often the currency of choice for those who had no cash.

That evening Rob gave Ramiza a small Bosnian New Testament. She studied it thoughtfully, occasionally asking questions but clearly not understanding the text. Confused, she put it down and shook her head as if wondering: *Where to start? How does one begin to read this little book?*

That night Annette and I lay in bed with Abigail cooing next to us, discussing all we had seen that day. Could this be our home? Was it safe enough for a family with five small children? Could we find a home? More important was the question we left unsaid: What do we have to offer these people?

During the siege it was difficult for the citizens of Sarajevo to tell their stories. The only news in and out of the city was filtered through the viewpoints of a superpower's 24-hour news staff, the U.N.'s press releases, and the army of foreign correspondents who were making names for themselves. Contrary to our expectation that people would not want to talk about their personal horrors, Sarajevans could hardly keep silent when given the opportunity to tell their own accounts. We had no way to tell the truthful stories from those that were being embellished, but after some time a pattern emerged that told an awful struggle for survival against one of the harshest of history's sordid tragedies.

We first met Mickey and Haji while searching for an apartment for Gary Levi, our co-worker. Mickey claimed that his apartment took the first direct hit in Dobrinja, an eastern suburb of high-rise residential buildings that lined the eastern side of the airport. As the tension was mounting, Serb tanks took control of the airport runway, and were prowling the tarmac and taxiways. From Mickey's first-floor apartment he and Haji could see a small sliver of the airport through the neighboring buildings. A tank paused in that opening and slowly swung its canon around in a slow arch. It stopped, pointing right at Mickey and Haji. They looked on puzzled, suddenly realizing in tandem that the tank was preparing to fire. As they dropped to the floor, the entire apartment erupted in flames and small projectiles. Amazingly, they were not hurt, but the entire face of the apartment was blown away, destroying any feeling of safety.

Mickey opened a small cafe in the days after the signing of the Dayton Peace Accords. As we sat with him and he reflected on his experiences, he pointed out the windows in which he had spent many days and nights as a sniper, looking down on the streets closest to the Serb positions. He proudly showed us his 4-year-old car. It had less than 3,000 miles on it. He purchased it days before the fighting began. One bullet hole in the windshield was enough to convince him to store it away in an underground garage. Unlike most treasures that was bartered away during the siege, Mickey had somehow managed to keep it so that it emerged four years later as a new car.

A few hundred feet from Mickey's cafe was a plaque dedicated to the memory of one of the many crowds of people who used the cover of the apartment buildings to fill their jugs of water at a well. During the siege these watering holes were among the most dangerous places in Sarajevo. Unknown to the lengthening line of young people, mothers, fathers, and elderly men and women, Serb mortar gunners had sighted this very spot during the cover of night. They were waiting for a crowd to gather before launching their deadly surprise. The shell hit its target in a huge shower of shrapnel and an echoing boom fell to a short moment of silence before agonized groans, crying, and the screaming of small children filled the air. The Serbs began to jeer at the wounded as loved ones poured out of buildings to fetch the dead and wounded, only to also be killed and maimed. Twelve people died that morning and 15 others were wounded.

Twelve people died that morning and 15 others were wounded.

In this city filled with tall apartment buildings and a working water system, everyone had to make a daily trip to fetch water. In some places, citizens fought by digging trenches where snipers otherwise had a clear shot. From the upper stories of a building, one could look down on these crude causeways that offered some semblance of safety. People set out into these civilian, survival trenches with plastic jugs that were supplied by the U.N. and allowed into the city by permission of the Serbs. The precious containers were tied together and strung over one's neck. A trip to the well meant exposing oneself to the snipers and possible mortar shells. After retrieving and retreating in utmost haste, people would stop to catch their breath in the safety of a stairwell before carrying their heavy treasure up flights of stairs.

During winter, cold proved as much a risk as thirst. After the family furniture was burned, fuel still had to be found. It was attainable the first winter of the siege, but by the next year, trees in the parks and greenways were cut down and hauled away. By the third winter, just about anything that could burn had been removed. The city was naked and barren.

Time and time again a Sarajevan would take us by the hand and ask us to listen. One story was about a son that escaped across the airport tarmac, only to return later at gunpoint by a Bosnian soldier. (It was not in the Bosnians' military interest to abandon Sarajevo.) Another was of a brave husband, shot down returning home after fighting just a few miles from home. Other stories were of the defiance of a single tank commandeered in the first weeks of fighting by citizen soldiers. We heard repeatedly of snipers living among the apartment complexes, shooting once every few weeks, and hiding out in the meantime, nobody quite certain which neighbors were, in fact, the enemy. Each story told of unspeakable atrocity.

Each story reminded us anew of the darkness of man's heart.

Chapter 4

MEET the LION

—•—

"You don't really suppose, do you, that all your adventures and escapes were managed by mere luck, just for your fine benefit? You are a very fine person, Mr. Baggins, and I am very fond of you; but you are only quite a little fellow in a wide world after all!"

—J.R.R. Tolkien, *The Hobbit*

On the east end of Sarajevo, high on a hill overlooking the city stands a fortress. The original part was built by the Turks, but like so many things in the Balkans, the Austrians have contributed to it as well. The resulting effect is that you can stand next to it and easily envision 16th-century Turkish soldiers walking patrol along the perimeter one minute and the next moment imagine the white stallions of the Austrian troops as they pick their way up from the mountainside below. It is one of those extraordinary places that lends itself to profound decisions and deep thoughts.

During the war, the Sarajevo Orchestra grabbed a window of calm created by a negotiated ceasefire to gather in this place. They played music within the shadows of the fortress as they did before the siege. Clicking news cameras accompanied their protest and helped make the point. Despite the ceasefire, the occasional sound of a machine gun or mortar shell punctuated the lulls and created a surreal impression. It was a concert of defiance that lifted the spirits of the city and gave the citizens hope that not all civilization had died.

One afternoon I found myself looking out from this historic spot. Minarets punctuated the skyline of the city and I could see the whole length of the city. The old Turkish library, still standing but gravely wounded, anchored the old part of town called Bascarsija. This Turkish name literally means "the exact center" and conveys a Sarajevan's view of the city in the same way that Times Square resounds with a New Yorker. The Miljacka River snaked its way down the valley, as if it were the backbone, and the many bridges, some of them broken in the middle, made a row of ribs.

On the hills that rose up to meet the fortress there were cemeteries. Not the old cemeteries filled with fine marble tombstones—small dirt mounds with Muslim grave markers carefully erected at one end. Flowers, wild and fresh, were placed on many of the graves. These were cemeteries created in the midst of a siege. They were placed where parks and playgrounds once hosted the laughter of small children and the romance of young lovers. The bodies couldn't be carried out, so a solution had to be found. Unlike the "stadium graveyard" that transformed the Olympic stadium into a temporary morgue until the end of the fighting, these cemeteries were here to stay.

Looking down on this landscape, I realized there was more to this city's suffering than I would ever understand. Again, the question of communicating Christ's love was overwhelming. It was not a place where "Christ had not been named." No, He was named many times and often accused of being the perpetrator of this war. Indeed, this was in some twisted way a religious war. Yet, Christ needed to be seen for who He really is.

I needed to learn—along with all of Sarajevo—that Jesus was all too eager to reveal Himself.

I needed to learn—along with all of Sarajevo—that Jesus was all too eager to reveal Himself.

Not long after our family arrived in Sarajevo we met Snahid. Some mutual friends made our acquaintance, and we began to see him regularly. In the early days of the church Annette would play the keyboard, and I would preach a short message. Our family alone literally tripled the size of the fellowship. This little church continued to meet throughout the war but it now consisted of just three or four people. Snahid's inclusion, even though he wasn't a follower of Christ, meant that we could have a Bosnian lead the music, and so we jumped at the possibility.

He would come and play guitar and participate in the meeting, hearing what was taught each week. We came to think of him as one of us, and even though he had a Muslim background, we believed that he was a Christian. Numerous conversations confirmed our conclusion.

The first winter that we were in Sarajevo we heated our home by wood. Prior to the war there was central heating by way of hot water pumped into the neighborhood. Now, the radiators stood coldly by while we fed the wood stove throughout the day. Because the homes are not constructed with air vents, each room needs its own heating source. I will never forget our colleagues who rose in the morning to break the ice that had formed in their toilet bowl the night before! Our hallways were be-low freezing on many cold nights while the kitchen and bedrooms (which had space heaters) would be toasty warm.

The first winter wood was hard to come by. The natural routines of the seasons were interrupted by the fighting such that precious little wood was prepared the summer before. The little that was available was "rough cut" in large logs too big for our wood stove. We decided to hire Snahid to cut wood for us. We gave him a couple hundred German marks (the de facto currency in Bosnia) and with it he could purchase the wood, rent a chainsaw, split the wood, and have some left for him. Micro-enterprise in a small package!

A week went by, and I hadn't heard from Snahid. I found out that we weren't the only ones to have hired him. Another week went past and Snahid still hadn't shown up—not in church, not at our home, and curiously, he was never home when I called on the telephone. With some consternation, I went down to his apartment and knocked on the door.

I heard Snahid's muffled footsteps as he came toward the door. The latch clicked and his face appeared in the crack—for a brief second—before the door quickly shut. Unfortunately for Snahid, he was battling culture.

East Europeans are so hospitable that I couldn't imagine that he would be able to leave me standing outside the door. Another click sounded and slowly the door swung open. Snahid looked down at the ground and mumbled, *"Sto ima?"* ("What's up?"). "Let's go for some coffee," I said, tapping the cultural laws that govern Bosnian interaction. He was trapped.

The engine of Bosnian society is fueled by coffee. When one wants to talk about something, whether it's the latest sports score or the current status of the war, one does so while drinking coffee. Hot cups of Turkish coffee were soon placed in front of us and Snahid slowly stirred the heavy foam on top with his spoon. Not once did he look at me. After a few minutes of trying to make small talk, I asked him what happened to the wood. There was no response, and I asked him where the money was. The entire time he avoided eye contact, and each question brought little more than a grunt or a slow bob of his head. He wasn't about to discuss anything with me. Attacking it from every angle, I wrestled to get a confession out of him. Finally, in exasperation, I said: "Forget about the wood and the money, Snahid. All you have to do is ask for forgiveness and I will forget about it all!" He continued to stare straight forward and look at the swirling foam in his cup of coffee.

I sat back for a few minutes letting the silence work on his conscience, hoping, wanting, and expecting Snahid to break the silence and the impasse we reached. After time had seemed to stand still for far too long, I blurted, "OK, forget about it! I forgive you." Still more stony silence. "I want you to know that I will never mention this again if you just let us be friends again as we once were."

Just a few bubbles still swirled in the foam of his coffee. Snahid stared, but said nothing. How will he ever hear the gospel if he doesn't let me speak with him? I wondered. I tried again. "We're having Bible study at our house on Wednesday night if you care to come." More silence. I stood up, threw some money down on the table and walked out.

Annette was saddened to hear about the conversation. Both of us spoke about the hatred we had seen since arriving in Sarajevo and concluded that once again, these were people who simply could not understand forgiveness. Just as the words of Serbo-Croatian were absolutely incomprehensible for us until we studied them at length, forgiveness was a foreign concept in this city and that would take time to learn. Or, so I thought.

The next Wednesday night Annette and I arranged the chairs in our living room, situated the kids in their rooms with books and toys, and began making the coffee. One by one they came, Blazenka, Miljenko, Silvana, Nena, and others filled the room. Just as we were about to start, a knock at the door brought Snahid. I was, to be honest, a bit more than surprised. He said nothing and took his place around the circle of chairs as we opened the Bible together. Quietly observing everything, he left that night with a smile and a promise to return the next week.

Since the power wasn't too reliable, there was always a ready supply of candles, and the next week found us sitting around the living room with our shadows flickering on the walls. Someone asked, "Who memorized the verse?" Only one hand shot up. Snahid quickly rattled off 1 John 5:11 and 12: "And the testimony is this, that God has given us eternal life, and this life is in His Son. He who has the Son has life; he who does not have the Son of God does not have the life." Annette and I quickly locked eyes across the room in a moment of praise!

Snahid was a silent participant for the rest of the evening. Still, hope returned to both Annette and I, and we doubled our prayer for him.

As the next few weeks went by, Snahid continued to participate in the Bible study. He was really learning and growing. About two months after our conversation in the café, we gathered for the study as usual. One of the exercises in the study guide was to tell everybody else where they were in their spiritual journey. One by one each person spoke of how they came to hear the story of Jesus and His death on the cross and how their lives were changed when they believed in Him. As we went from person to person, there was an air of expectation mixed with concern at what Snahid might say. As it drew near to Snahid's turn, he grew pensive and thoughtful. I thought he would ask to be skipped, but instead he came alive.

"I heard Jesus explained many times, but I didn't really understand what it all meant. I first understood what God did for us when Ted forgave me. I wasn't even asking forgiveness, but Ted sought me out even though I was trying to avoid him." He went on to tell everybody what had transpired between us. As he continued he said, "Even then, I was stubborn and would not admit that I had stolen from him. But he forgave me just the same. Not only that, he invited me to come back to this Bible study, held in his home. I had to decide if I would take Ted's forgiveness or reject it. I have been brought up to be a Muslim. Muslims aren't taught much about forgiveness. This was the first time that I really saw forgiveness. This is what God has done for us. Even though we deserve to be punished for our sins He has provided forgiveness. Even though we are stubborn and try to avoid God, He looks for us. It's up to us to reject His forgiveness or accept it. I have chosen to accept His forgiveness. I know what Jesus has done for me. I understand what God has done."

My eyes welled up with tears as I saw how God used the events to so plainly and simply lead Snahid to himself. It was a revelation of how God works—sometimes despite the efforts of His servants and their inadequate attempts "to minister." I never intended for that discussion regarding stolen wood to be about salvation. In fact, that conversation stood out to me as a failure: Snahid didn't even seem to be listening. God knew what kind of lesson Snahid needed, and He provided it.

Even in a place filled with so much hatred and strife, God speaks. The Lion of Judah roars life into the souls of men in a language far more effective than my faltering words. Looking back, I consider Snahid's decision to follow Christ my first lesson in sharing Christ. I was in school that first year in Sarajevo—learning from the Master how He loves His people.

— ❧❧ —

CHAPTER 5

MACHINE GUNS
AND
SWING SETS

—

"Love them in."
—D. L. MOODY

"Do you think that Sarajevo would like to have a playground?" asked Denny Johnson.

I immediately invited Denny, Jim Rosene, and Ralph Peterson from Kids Around the World to Sarajevo to investigate the possibilities. This unique organization is built on a powerfully simple concept: Christians can show love to kids by building playgrounds for them. They literally give away playgrounds to distressed communities all around the world. Not only do they donate the materials necessary to build the playgrounds, they assemble teams of volunteers who, along with local labor, install the equipment. Not only do they finance and plan the project, but they also work alongside the local churches and missionaries to ensure that the "good works" are done in the name of Christ.

Denny and Ralph arrived a few weeks later, in the spring of 1996. Since the airport in Sarajevo was not yet open, we often drove to Zagreb to meet visitors. I shipped a blue Chrysler mini-van from the U.S. that led to the somewhat surreal experience of driving this "suburban cruiser" amidst the tanks, Jeeps, personnel carriers, and other military vehicles that were on the road. Bosnia had not yet issued its own license plates, so this van still carried Minnesota tags.

After picking up Denny and Ralph, we headed east along the Sava River until we came to the ferry crossing just north of Tuzla, in the shadow of a huge destroyed bridge that used to be the main highway between eastern Croatia and Bosnia. At that time the road that led south cut directly through a NATO checkpoint at the U.S. military base. Later, it wound through a stretch controlled by Serb irregulars. Ominously nicknamed "The Corridor," it was the route considered to be the shortest between Croatia and Bosnia that offered at least some safety. We often heard stories about problems on this shortcut but decided to give it a try.

Pulling up to the checkpoint a heavily armed U.S. Army soldier approached our vehicle. He stopped and stared for a few moments before reaching up and slowly lowering his sunglasses to peer at us with a quizzical expression. A smile broke out over his face, and he loudly asked: "Hey Minnesota, what ch' ya doin' here? Ya'll done took a wrong turn at Iowa!" As he checked our ID cards the suburban cruiser was filled with giggles and snorts—an adventure had begun.

Driving along this route into Sarajevo offered Denny and Ralph plenty of opportunity to see the destruction that war brings. Homes were burnt and pillaged, many spray-painted with the large Serbian swastika. Posters with the grim face of Slobodan Milosevic (the Serbian president nicknamed the "Butcher of the Balkans") graced billboards and bus stops. As we entered the actual "corridor"—the Serbian section of Bosnia—the trees grew out into the road on each side, evidence that the area had been no-man's land during the last few years. Whole villages had been razed to the ground and deserted. We passed gas stations which had been reduced to broken pavement and twisted metal stumps where the pumps used to stand. The levity and safety we felt at the military base quickly gave way to the seriousness and reality that people's lives had been destroyed at the hands of other people in this place. The Serbs were suffering as well.

As we finally entered Sarajevo, Denny noted that a playground would certainly get people's attention. *Wow, I thought to myself, these guys have no clue...* Survivors dreamed of daily essentials. Who could have imagined the gift of recreation?

Denny, a former city council member from Rockford, Illinois, met with the city officials while Ralph scoped out the proposed site. Of all the potential locations, Dobrinja stood out as the best option. A more recent addition to the city of Sarajevo, it was constructed a few decades earlier as a means to relieve congestion in the downtown core of the city. Known as a "white collar" community, it was home to close to 20,000 people living in high-rise apartment buildings.

During the war, this part of town became an early focal point. It was literally a siege within a siege. In the initial fighting, the Serbs took the hills that lined Dobrinja, as well as the airport that bordered the western edge of the suburb. The Muslims had taken the northernmost strip that ended where "Sniper Alley" started.

Since Sniper Alley was exposed to the hills, the only way in and out of Dobrinja was under the cover of darkness.

While many people in Sarajevo eventually were able to get some supplies of food and humanitarian aid via the United Nations or other government sources, Dobrinja could not. Facing the worst of war, the people in Dobrinja formed their own civil defense unit and organized themselves for survival. Even during the most brutal days of fighting they were able to keep a postal system running while makeshift schools met in the darkened basements of the apartment complexes. Municipal offices were kept open for most of the siege. The entire suburb was mapped out and a system of trenches was strategically dug into the ground to connect the buildings. One could walk, hunched over, all across Dobrinja with minimal exposure to sniper fire. A small river cuts through Dobrinja, effectively cutting it in half. This was a danger point since the bridges were exposed to the hills. Smashed cars were flattened and used to line these bridges making a more secure route. Piles of cars were also set up as barricades in front of entrances to buildings, around corners, and at other exposure points in the community. A makeshift hospital was built in the basement level of one of the buildings. In that one hospital, thousands of people were treated. The doctors that staffed this hospital are true heroes for how they served during this very difficult time.

Even so, the siege was so tight that people were beginning to starve. It was decided that they would need to build a tunnel stretching to the outside world. On the far side of the airport, the Muslim army held Mount Igman. They selected a house, knocked a hole in the cement floor, and dug a tunnel that went underneath the entire airport, coming up at the base of the mountain on the far side. The population of Sarajevo passed through the tunnel many times over during the two-plus years it was open. The military used it for troop movement, food was brought in and out, and the black market thrived as the prices of coffee and cigarettes soared. Many needing to get in or out of the tunnel paid a stiff toll. Since the tunnel was only about 4½-feet tall, determined Sarajevans stooped at the waist and walked laden with bundles for the mile or so journey. The bottom of the tunnel began to fill with water after a few months, and passage was not a pleasant experience. My short trip into the tunnel made me wonder how anybody could carry anything in it, let alone the heavy packs and boxes that many claimed they carried.

Local folklore recounts a tale that the Serbs knew it was there and tried to find it. The United Nations had control of the airport tarmac, and the Serbs were not allowed to dig directly down to the tunnel. From one side of the airport they began their own tunneling effort in hopes of finding the Muslim's underground highway. As the story goes, they began to cut across the airport when they hit an underground spring, instantly filling their efforts with water. There is little doubt that great effort went into finding this thin lifeline to the world.

At each end of the tunnel were houses that served as the entrances. Understandably, the Serbs heavily shelled these houses. On the Sarajevo side of the tunnel, an extension was dug into the apartment complexes. One teammate's apartment was across from a small parking lot and an open space. Gary Levi could see the tunnel opening from his living room window. It was a visible reminder that his neighbors fought creatively for life itself. In front of Gary's building, in the open space, there were a number of graves. The graves were put there when there was no way to get bodies in or out of Dobrinja. As one made their way through Dobrinja, many of the little townhouse units had small backyards with one or two graves in them.

Looking out of Gary's apartment to the left, you could see the opening to a new tunnel, dug after the first one was completed. Since nobody knew how many years the siege would continue, the Bosnian army built a second, much larger tunnel with rails running through it. It was to be used to get goods in and out of the city more easily than the first one, but the war ended the week it opened.

Right in the middle of Dobrinja is an open field with buildings on three sides. The main market—a daily source of groceries, fresh vegetables, coffee shops, and town gossip—sits to one side of the field. The city offered this field for the playground. USAID (United States Agency for International Development) was willing to provide some support to the project, and the local municipality was very interested in seeing things go forward. Obviously there were no longer any places for kids to play, and it was a highly populated area. The decision was made to build here, and Denny and Ralph returned to the U.S. to make preparations.

In late August, the first shipments of equipment began arriving. Kids Around the World purchases a complete set of playground equipment as well as all of the tools necessary to put it together and ships them to the installation site. Getting more than $100,000 of playground equipment into a place like Bosnia was itself an adventure. The U.S. Armed Forces stepped in to help out, providing all the transportation free of charge. As a part of the Dayton Peace Accord, NATO implemented a plan called "Arms for Bosnia." They were training and arming the Bosnian military to create a military balance between them and the Serbs. Millions of dollars of military hardware began arriving in huge transport planes.

Packed alongside the machine guns, armored vehicles, and other weapons were purple slides, swings, and merry-go-rounds.

Each crate was carefully packed with all of the tools that would be needed for the job. Nails, screwdrivers, rakes, brooms, shovels, picks, wheelbarrows, hammers, wrenches, and an endless assortment of nuts and bolts was placed into these numbered crates for easy access. The organization was astounding. One rather large rectangular crate was outfitted with a hinged top. The top was opened up and the contents were taken out and checked against a manifest. As the power tools and other items were lifted out, a toilet was revealed, bolted onto the bottom of the box. A saw was produced, and a hole surgically cut in the wood where the toilet had been bolted

Packed alongside the machine guns, armored vehicles, and other weapons were purple slides, swings, and merry-go-rounds.

on. Setting the crate on end produced an instant out-house, complete with a door and toilet, ready to place at the construction site.

One problem that arose concerned sand. Most play-grounds in the West use sand as the ground-covering material in the playground area. Typically Kids Around the World would arrange ahead of time to have sand brought to the worksite. The Bosnians didn't think this was a good idea. Sand is a primary ingredient in cement. Since so many of the buildings were shelled, there was a severe shortage of cement. It was quickly calculated that if each resident hauled off just one bucket of sand, there would be none left for the playground. The U.S. Army Corps of Engineers provided the solution. They suggested that sand be hauled in from the Adriatic coast. With its high salt content, people would quickly learn that it was useless for making cement. Trucks were dis-patched and returned hours later. As they dumped the very first load of sand, a number of older gentlemen car-rying shovels and buckets descended onto the mounds. When they were informed that this sand was from the sea, they gave us a hard stare and walked away. The sand would be for the kids.

Since 5-foot deep trenches circled the playground area (a part of the civil defense plan) the first step was to fill them in and level the field. Tons of dirt and debris were moved to create the volleyball court and outline the site for the playground equipment. The city of Sarajevo provided a bulldozer that broke down on the second day. Unfortunately, the tight schedule required that each phase of the project be completed before the next could begin. The team would only be in country for eight or nine days. An alternative plan had to be found. As men from the community were recruited, I was sent downtown with a wad of money. I returned with 20 shovels after purchasing the entire inventory at the first and only hardware store in Sarajevo at the time. Everyone was assigned a shovel, and they went to work digging and moving all that dirt by hand—along with tons and tons of sand.

Another problem occurred when the ground began tearing apart the gasoline-powered posthole diggers. Many of the playground pieces required a deep foundation, and the hand diggers were found unusable as well. I was sent to the American Embassy, where the Embassy was digging deeply underground to create a potential "war-time Embassy," should the fighting start anew. They provided us with a specialized machine that could eat through the hardened surface.

The city of Dobrinja had one paid employee: Dana.

She first met Denny and Ralph during the exploratory trip some months earlier. Without Dana's help, this project simply would not have been possible. She knew who to call, where resources could be found, and was not afraid to tell people to pitch in and help.

During the whole process of construction, anticipation among the kids was rising. Early on, a plastic orange fence was erected around the perimeter of the construction zone. It was intended to keep the kids out during the building process, but this became more and more difficult. A crowd of children would form early in the morning and keenly observe all that was going on. On a number of occasions a child would break through the fence and come walking in to get a closer view of the action. It didn't take long to get quite familiar with a number of them. Most were displaced refugees, moved into Dobrinja to take the empty flats of Serbs and Croats who fled in the early days of the war.

Redjo left a mark on my heart that will be with me forever. He was from Srebrenica where terrible mass executions occurred. Redjo's father had, in fact, been killed in one of these massacres. His mother was working to make ends meet, living in Dobrinja as a squatter in a flat left behind by a fleeing Serb family. Redjo was basically alone all day long—a hard thing for a 6-year-old. To see the playground being formed in the field right out of his apartment window was more than thrilling for him. All I needed to do was to look at him and smile, and he would start laughing.

By the sixth day most of the major pieces were in place. Chains were hung on the steal frames of the swing sets. The foundation for the merry-go-round was finished, and the large circular plate was being bolted into place. The multi-colored plastic pieces for the slides were lying in large heaps as workers checked installation instructions and began assembling them.

That day a story was run on the Serbian TV station, describing the playground. It was being built on the Muslim side of the Dayton Peace Accords' "line of demarcation" but the Serbs could easily see it from where they were. In fact, they filmed it and stated that it was an example of the unfair distribution of rebuilding resources by the international community. They declared that people in the Serbian Republic were still without electricity and other basic needs—and here we were building a playground. I felt the irony that so disturbed them as well. They didn't, however, know all that was going on.

What they didn't know was that while the playground was being built, a plastic surgeon, who came with the playground team, was busy repairing the face of a small child. The German aid organization, Hifle Konkret, led by Johannes Neudeck, in cooperation with the Croatian relief organization My Neighbor, delivered tons of food to the site and it was being distributed to the residents. A team of puppeteers was ministering in the local schools, and others distributed hundreds of copies of Billy Graham's book *Peace With God* in the community. We would have loved to include the Serbs in this project, but they were not open to our involvement on their side of the line. There would be a time for that, but it would come a few years later.

As the playground took shape and was nearing completion, the crowd of children grew substantially. Thankfully, school started, and there was some relief from the eager inquiries of "when will it be done?" I heard a little voice say in Bosnian, "It looks like Disney Land."

On the opening day, the children from the Dobrinja School surrounded the playground and sang a song of thanks to the team that came to build the playground. The mayor of Dobrinja spoke and then my turn came. I said a few words of thanks and had the opportunity to explain the motivation behind these people who came to serve Dobrinja. They came to share out of their abundance because God shared with them out of His abundance. The ribbon was cut, and the playground was over-whelmed with children. In the next four or five days about 30,000 children flooded the playground. They were arriving by bus from all over Sarajevo and the outlying villages. In the first week or two, they compacted the sand and dirt so much that it was as hard as rock!

Kids Around the World taught a lesson. Not to Sa-rajevo or to the Muslims, but to me. Showing love opens doors. While I certainly knew that truth intellectually, here was a concrete (and plastic) example of it. A num-ber of people experienced the stirrings of the Holy Spirit as they saw evidence of God. This was not scientific evi-dence, of course. No, it was much more powerful and convincing than that.

A few weeks later I applied for a residency permit from the Bosnian government. Gary Levi and I went to the police station and inquired about the process. "Well," stated the man behind the desk, "nobody has ever asked us that before." We had the blessing of be-ing the first foreigners to apply for residency! As we entered the Muslim interrogator's office, we were a bit concerned about Gary's Jewish last name. As he sized us up and got our names down on paper, he stopped in mid-sentence. Sticking his pen out at us like a scabbard, he asked us if we had anything to do with that playground in Dobrinja. "Yes, we did." We had our papers in just a few minutes along with a command to come see him if we had any problems.

Sitting on a park bench one afternoon Annette and I watched our kids scramble all over the equipment. Redjo was there, of course, sharing the tire swing with our son, David. I reflected how, in just a few short weeks, God moved our family into Sarajevo and enabled us to establish many relationships with people in this wounded city. A Bible study was meeting, and God was blessing. It was time to gather the believers into a church.

— ⟨≈⟩ —

Chapter 6

BY THIS
ALL MEN
WILL KNOW

—◆—

"A new commandment I give to you, that you love one another,
even as I have loved you, that you also love one another.
By this all men will know that you are My disciples, if you have
love for one another." —Jesus, John 13:34-35

One by one they swept through the cobblestone
streets past small cafés and open shops. They passed by
men with small red hats who sat in clusters on wooden
benches circling low wooden tables, puffing hand-rolled
cigarettes while sipping strong cups of black coffee. The
misty fog of the city settled down heavy on Ferhadija

Street, where this first group of evangelical Christians gathered to sing and pray together. The year was 1866, and these believers, mostly from Germany, were among the first missionaries to live in Sarajevo. Their church would not be large, but it would certainly stand the test of time.

These brave believers were actually well ahead of their time. They were colporteurs—missionaries who supported their ministry on the sale of Bibles. They were true pioneers. It would be decades before the evangelical world would take note of the Muslim world and begin sending tentmakers where doors are closed.

In 1866, Sarajevo was on the far Western edge of the Turkish Ottoman Empire. The Turks came to power in what is now Bosnia in the 1500s. However, throughout the 1800s, their power waned. In 1877, Russia dealt a deadly military blow to the Turks and this forced the Ottomans to let go of their Balkan kingdom. At the Congress of Berlin in 1878, the European powers gave Bosnia to the Hapsburgs. The small Baptist fellowship struggled to survive in the transition from the Turks to the Hapsburgs. They were forced from their rented space and began meeting in the members' homes. The new rulers of Bosnia, the Catholic Austrians, were no more inclined to Baptists than they were to Muslims.

In 1914, Serb nationalist Gavrillo Princip assassinated Archduke Franz Ferdinand. Austria, ready to take on Serbia, declared war. Serbia called on Russia's help while Germany came in on Austria's side. France and Britain eventually were drawn in on the Serbian/Russian side of the war. Turkey also got involved, hoping to get back some of the Balkan territory it had lost. World War I, born on the streets of Sarajevo, claimed millions of lives. It all started just a few hundred yards from the small fellowship of believers, quietly seeking to change the world another way.

In 1918, Yugoslavia came into existence as "The Kingdom of Serbs, Croats, and Slovenes." Within its borders were 13 distinct languages. Serbs ruled without much apparent concern for the rest of the Yugoslav population. When World War II started, Croatian nationalists saw alignment with Germany as their only hope of establishing an independent Croatia. Unfortunately, many Serbs were killed at the hands of Croatian fascists. A resistance movement grew that was called "The Partisans," led by Josip Broz. Broz, whom we know as Tito, became the hero of a united Yugoslavia. At the end of World War II, Tito led Yugoslavia in a new direction—communism. Once again the small Baptist church faced a formidable foe. As Tito's regime purged Germans from Yugloslavia, the makeup of the church changed dramatically.

It was during this time that the fellowship moved to a part of Sarajevo called Grbavica. Meeting in the basement of a house on Ljubljanska Street, the church was not unlike its counterparts in other communist lands. It was a small, faithful, and tightly knit group. Made up primarily of Serbs and Croats, it was unable to make great inroads into society as a whole. However, in all of Bosnia it was one of a handful of evangelical churches that went against the tide of communism.

During the 1980s, the Baptist church began a new effort to reach out to Muslim Sarajevo. They purchased a building in the main Muslim quarter of Sarajevo, in Bascarsija. A sign was placed over the door that read "The House of Prayer for All Nations." The Serbian pastor didn't know just how much this statement would contrast with the politics of division that would descend upon Sarajevo just a few years after the world watched Olympic athletes compete in this city.

In the beginning days of the war, Sarajevo was almost immediately surrounded. The Serbs hoped that Sarajevo could become the capital of a new Serbian-dominated Bosnia. Their initial aim was to keep the city fairly intact. As the resistance grew, it became obvious that Sarajevo would not simply surrender. The Serb hesitation became a fatal mistake and kept them from overtaking the city, but the small Bosnian army, poorly armed and supplied, could not break the siege. With the end of the hostilities in 1996, the Sarajevo Baptist Church had but five or six members left alive in the city.

Soon after moving to Sarajevo we were asked by the Croatian Baptist Union if we would help to re-establish this congregation. The Union held the deeds for two properties and needed to have a representative in the area to ensure that these pieces of land would not be grabbed in the tidal wave of ownership changes that mass migration brings. There was great flux in the city regarding land. Serbs and Croats who fled were losing their apartments to squatters, and the hundreds of Muslim refugees in Sarajevo were likewise losing their property in the villages that they came from. We knew that working in partnership with local movements was usually the best route to take, so we agreed and our association with the Sarajevo Baptist Church began.

Three elderly women were still meeting weekly. The women, Gary Levi, Annette, our kids, and I met for our first time of worship together. It was during the fall and there was no heat in the building. We worshiped in our jackets and parkas and though our noses were ice cold, our hearts were warm. We sang, prayed, and opened up the Bible together, rejoicing in our God and the purposes He had for this region. He was present, and it didn't matter that we were such a minority.

The local newspapers in both Croatia and Bosnia were running stories about the ethnic breakdown of each city and village. The idea, of course, was to show the European and American politicians that their people were either in the majority (in need of control) or in the minority (in need of protection). I couldn't help but think about what a tiny minority we were. Unlike the other minorities, the only weapon at our disposal was the love of Christ.

Many of the first people in the church came to us through the work of other Christians in the Balkans. Nena was a young woman who had grew up in Sarajevo. Since she carried a Serbian name, her family urged her to leave and go to Belgrade. Relatives there would surely receive her. Arriving in Belgrade she received an icy welcome and was not let into the house. Even though she was a Serb, she was a Bosnian, which was as bad as being a Muslim in the eyes of her relatives. They left her outside, as hungry and "penniless" as she arrived.

She found a girlfriend, also a refugee, and together they found a landlord that would rent a room to them in return for work. Each day they would work cleaning homes and other odd jobs as the landlord would find. Nena described it as a time of economic slavery. Whatever the lady said to do, they had to do. There was no additional money paid to them except room and board, and they saw no way out of their squalid conditions. Nena began to become depressed. One evening they were returning home from a day of labor and saw an advertisement that a church had put up. It was a simple poster with the simple challenge: "Does God love me? Come to this church to find out." Nena was raised as an atheist and never contemplated God before. "This might be interesting," she said to her friend, "Let's go and see what they have to say."

It was the first time Nena ever heard the gospel or anything like it. She immediately became a follower of Christ and began to grow in her walk with the Lord. Over the next 1½ years, she determined that God wanted her to return to Sarajevo and share this message with her friends. When the war finished that was exactly what she did.

Arriving in Sarajevo she found a city much different than the one she left. Her friends had all separated into their various ethnic subcultures and were no longer on speaking terms. Each time this young Serbian girl began sharing about Jesus, the Muslims gave her hard stares or worse. She was alone and without fellowship. The grapevine brought news to her that there were some people meeting in town with similar, unusual teachings about Jesus. One Sunday morning she introduced herself to me. She had brought along a friend who was not a believer and she asked if the three of us could meet together.

Sitting at a table in a café she told me her story. Her friend listened intently, sometimes shaking his head and smiling at her. She asked if she would be welcome to come, and be a part of the church and serve in the church. She then turned to the young man she brought and told him to listen to "Pastor" about Jesus. This was what Nena was all about: sharing Jesus with other people. She would meet people and immediately invite them to a Bible study, sharing her faith in the process. She became a faithful member of the Sarajevo fellowship.

Her story was not unlike another young woman we met, Silvana—although the outcomes of their lives would be tragically different. Silvana's family was mixed, her father was a Serb and her mother was a Croat. When she was a little girl her parents were divorced and her mother moved to Mostar, a few hours from Sarajevo. When the war started, Silvana left the city and found herself in Croatia as a refugee. In God's providence she enrolled in an English course taught by Christians. An eager student, Silvana learned much more than she anticipated. The team of teachers shared Christ with her, and Silvana became a believer in Christ. She remained in Croatia until the hostilities ended and the refugees were asked to return home.

When the fighting stopped, Croatia asked Bosnian refugees to leave the country since they were dealing with enough of their own problems. Silvana's mother, desperately ill and now living in Croatia, lay in the hospital. Silvana could not return to Mostar, so she moved to be with her father. He no longer lived in the family apartment since it was destroyed. He was squatting in an apartment that previously belonged to a Serbian family. A very strong-willed man, he gave Silvana little freedom, despite the fact that she was in her early 30s.

Silvana helped lead worship for our little fellowship before Snahid joined us. I would play guitar, Annette would play a little battery-powered keyboard and Silvana led the singing. This was no easy task for our Bosnian friend since she was terribly shy.

Every time Silvana left the apartment, she had to first ask permission from her parents before she could go. Coming to our house she and Annette would laugh and talk together, preparing food for a time of fellowship in our home, playing with the kids, or simply being friends. One day she told us that she was no longer allowed to come to church anymore or associate with Christians. More than once we visited her to make sure that she was all right. With sadness in her eyes she said she was OK and that we need not worry. She told us that she loved us and it was nothing personal, but she was unable to come right now and to pray for her.

Late one night Silvana went to the building that was her home as a child. The entire front face of the building was destroyed, exposing every room that faced the hills that housed Serb gun positions. Climbing the stairs to the top of the tall high-rise complex, life overtook Silvana. She edged close to the opening and lept out. We held the funeral two days later.

She edged close to the opening and lept out.

We held the funeral two days later.

We searched our hearts to understand this senseless act. Suicide rates in Sarajevo were high. People hung on as long as possible during the war and when it ended had high expectations that life would return to normal. With unemployment rates of 80 percent and little political stability except that coming from

NATO guns, life could not return to what it once was. A Serb living in Sarajevo faced many difficulties. Silvana had little opportunity for employment. Discrimination was the rule rather than the exception, even though the international community went to great lengths to protect minorities.

Silvana lived a life of quiet submission. Her family torn apart as a child, her mother dying in a nearby country and the stern hand of her father kept her from friends. This would be enough to push most people to despair. What would God say to her as she climbed toward heaven? I imagined something like this: "Come to me, child. I'm so sorry that your despair reached those depths. I'm so sorry it ended like that for you, but here's eternity before you in My presence and you don't need to be ashamed or embarrassed about what has happened, it is in the past."

It was the first time we had someone close to us, who was a part of our inner circle, do anything like this. She knew Jesus. In a country like Bosnia, where there are so few Christians, each and every one of them is precious. Silvana's suicide was even more senseless than it might be elsewhere. It struck our little fellowship hard.

Some time later, a small, diminutive man walked through the doors of the church and took a seat toward the back. He said nothing the whole morning, and when we finished, he vanished out the back door. This happened again the next week—he left so quickly that I couldn't catch him before he left. The third week I posted guards at the back to intercept him. When I introduced myself to him, he told me that he was a friend of the pastor in Daruvar. He asked if he could join with us, which of course was fine with us.

One day in the summer of 1993 Miljenko and a neighbor left their apartment building together. A shell exploded at his feet. His friend was killed immediately, and Miljenko was badly wounded. He was rushed down Sniper Alley to the hospital and eventually taken out of the city by the United Nations. Now a refugee, he found himself recuperating in a hospital in Croatia. After a few months he was asked to leave the hospital, but he had nowhere to go.

He decided to travel to another city in Croatia where his relatives were living. They were Serbs living in Croatia, and Croatia and Serbia were at war. When he appeared on the doorstep they told him to leave—they didn't want the neighbors to think that they were harboring Bosnian Serbs. They were Croats now and couldn't afford to be seen as Serb sympathizers. Identity cards were issued to those who qualified for official refugee status, but Miljenko, as a Serb, was denied. He found himself on the streets of Daruvar with nowhere to go, all of his worldly possessions carried in two plastic bags at his side. He walked the streets of the small town, scared, tired, and broken. He passed by the Baptist Church and noticed that they were distributing food to people. He timidly asked if he would be allowed to have some.

"Of course, brother!" said the pastor, wrapping his arms around Miljenko and asking his name. Miljenko hesitated, knowing that his name would identify him as a Serb. "Miljenko Popovic," he replied, looking down at the ground. "Well, Miljenko," replied the pastor without hesitation, "we are glad you are here and want to help you in any way we can." Over the next months the church provided him with food, assisted him with housing, and helped him with blankets and other items.

Miljenko spent most of his life as a member of the Communist Party. He was a veterinarian and had never known poverty or need. His life experience had never allowed him to fellowship with Christians before. He faithfully attended church and Bible studies, gobbling up all the teaching he could.

Arriving back in Sarajevo in the fall of 1996, Miljenko established a close friendship with Gary Levi. Gary is from a small town in Georgia. It was always fun for me to hear him speak Bosnian with a thick southern accent. It was even more fun to watch him and Miljenko carry on lengthy conversations; Miljenko speaking Bosnian, and Gary replying in English. They honestly thought they were connecting even though I understood both languages and knew they weren't! What was communicated between them was much more than mere words.

One cold winter day Miljenko called asking for an appointment with Gary and me. This got my attention. Typically, Miljenko would just show up. As we sat together he reached into his pocket and withdrew a letter. I remembered hearing about "Invitation Letters" given during the communist era. Since Christians were persecuted by the government, one could not simply show up in a new church and expect to be welcomed. So, a pastor would write a letter of invitation, and since the pastors usually knew each other, it was safe to welcome this new person.

The letter stated that Miljenko was being sent from the Baptist Church in Croatia, and that we were to receive him as a friend. It was dated almost a year prior— Miljenko carried this letter with him the whole time he was in Sarajevo but never gave it to me.

His voice cracked as he told us about how he left

Sarajevo and found acceptance among the believers in Croatia. When he returned to Bosnia he did not trust us; he thought that he would never again find the acceptance he experienced while a refugee in Croatia. "I am wrong," he said with tears welling up in his eyes, "The love I found in Croatia is what I have found here among you. I heard the teaching before, but I know now that the only thing in common between there and here is Jesus. I know it is Jesus who gives this love because I see how you two love each other. I would like to become a follower of Jesus and share in this love." We prayed together, and Miljenko hugged each of us. A lifetime of communism was undone by the power of love.

I assumed, since meeting Miljenko the first time, that he already was a believer in Christ. He knew the right things to say and do. But his suspicion of anything that smacked of religion was so strong that he was unable to let go of it. Two years later Miljenko died of old age. I praise God for the picture I have of him in my mind; sitting on our front balcony with Abigail in his arms, gently singing to her as she played with his face.

Miljenko taught me the truth that Jesus declares in the gospel of John. The love between believers is by far the strongest advertisement for the kingdom of

God. Serbs, Croats, and Muslims were beginning to see it, and one by one, God was building the fellowship in Sarajevo out of the ashes of war.

LUCKY STRIKES

"A dog in desperation will leap over a wall."
—CHINESE PROVERB

War creates a desperation in people that knows few boundaries. Morality rapidly plummets as opportunities for such things as food and clothing diminishes. Satan is well aware of this dynamic, and even after the physical cease-fire, we were often aware that the war continued in spiritual proportions.

One Friday in 1997, I drove a group of four people to an annual conference held by the leadership of the churches in Croatia and Bosnia. It was a long, 10-hour drive through the mountains and somebody lent us a Land Rover to make the trip.

While we were driving north that day, Annette opened up our garage and was distributing a shipment of shoes that were delivered to us by a team from another mission agency. People streamed in from all over Sarajevo to look through the various sizes of shoes and find something that would fit them. Unfortunately, distributions of humanitarian aid are seldom easy and never fun. When people live in poverty, they take every opportunity to not only get their needs met, but also to plan ahead for the eventual reality of not having enough again. Some of the people were bending the rules as far as they could, taking shoes for unknown relatives and children they never had. We joked at times, watching some walked away looking fairly lumpy. Mary Jo Fletcher, one of our team members, joined Annette to assist with crowd control.

A scream rang out from outside the garage, and somebody began urgently calling for Annette. As she ran out of the garage door she found our son Joshua laying on the cement driveway unconscious. He was walking along the retaining wall next to the driveway and fell six feet onto the concrete surface, directly onto his head. For the first moments he was incoherent and unable to talk, focus his eyes, or walk. As Mary Jo rushed to see what was happening, Joshua began to go into spastic seizures as horror engulfed the onlookers.

Picking him up and moving him to our van, they

called Bill Deans from the relief organization Samaritan's Purse. The hospitals in Sarajevo were severely damaged and so Samaritan's Purse organized an effort to refurbish the Intensive Care Unit at The State Hospital in downtown Sarajevo. The renovations ran well into the hundreds of thousands of dollars. I am not sure where they would have taken Joshua without this tremendous gift from the organization led by Franklin Graham.

As my wife and teammate drove toward downtown, Bill got into his vehicle and drove toward them. Meeting under the bombed-out hulk of the newspaper building, together they loaded Joshua into Bill's vehicle and raced through the streets of Sarajevo together. Bill immediately took them to the Intensive Care Unit. Like any hospital, one isn't supposed to admit oneself to ICU, but Bill wasn't in the mood to wait. When the guard at the front desk saw Bill coming in carrying Joshua, he got out of his way.

By God's grace, the doctor who had been instrumental in overseeing the Samaritan's Purse project was the only neurosurgeon in the whole of Bosnia. He was the man who brought the hospital's need to the attention of Samaritan's Purse. When Bill called him, he came immediately. A CT scan revealed that Joshua had quite a bit of swelling in his brain, and the doctor said the situation was critical. For the next couple of hours Joshua drifted in and out of consciousness as Annette and Bill intently watched.

They called the conference center in Croatia, and I received the message to call home. By this time, Joshua spoke but the swelling was not abating. There was concern that his heart could stop due to pressure that was continuing to build in and around the base of his brain.

I got back into the Land Rover and started the drive back. Traveling at night in Bosnia was not a good idea that soon after the fighting. A curfew was still in place and numerous checkpoints were set up. One section of the road was closed off, and I had to drive down into the woods among the landmine warning tape that lined each side of the road. I arrived about 5:30 a.m. and went to the hospital to see Joshua.

He improved some, but he was still in critical condition, on a monitor, and very uncomfortable. When we first walked in he was in a daze and crying out asking, "When can I go home?" Noises from the various machines were frightening him. The man in the bed next to his was on a respirator, and every now and then the man would gag on the tube. Joshua asked me if the man was going to die.

Fortunately, the major danger passed and that day

he had a number of visitors. The next morning found him talking about a sore shoulder and we discovered a huge lump on his collarbone. It broke when he fell. After four days of observation, they released him. The staff was amazed that he didn't have permanent brain damage. The international fellowship of Pioneers had interceded. Christians in many nations around the world, in some cases meeting in churches that were among the first churches in that culture, were praying for Joshua. Even years later I meet national believers in far away places that say, "Years ago we prayed for an American boy in Sarajevo..."

The next week there was a knock at our door, and Annette opened it to find Srecko. His name means Lucky, but he was anything but Lucky. He was coming to the church on and off for a couple of weeks. We heard his story from others in the church. His wife and a couple of his children were killed during the war, leaving him and his son alone in the world. He was dressed very poorly, was always dirty, and had a hard time talking clearly. Like most people in Bosnia, he chain smoked and had a hard time waiting for the service to end so that he could satisfy his habit outside on the street.

About three days after Joshua left the hospital, Lucky came to our home. He heard about the shoe distribution and came to ask Annette if there were any shoes left. By then we had given away almost all of the shoes. He then asked for some money. We typically resisted giving people money. People asking for money approached us quite often and if we ever gave it to them they repeatedly came back for more. Looking at his feet, Annette knew his request for help was serious—his shoes were in terrible shape. She went into the garage and found something that fit him. He gratefully took it.

The next day he came back and once again asked for money. Annette wanted to know why he needed the money, and he said that his child was sick and in the hospital, and he needed it to buy medications for the child. Images of a small boy lying in the ICU came to her mind. The story sounded a little suspicious, though, and Annette was afraid to help him without first checking the story out. She sent him away without anything.

He came again the next morning. He looked worse than usual. Annette greeted him and once again he asked for money. Annette said: "I told you yesterday, you can't have any money. Please don't come begging for money." She then asked how his son was, and he looked at her and said, "He died early this morning." He went on to explain that the boy was struck by a car and after a few days in the hospital had passed on.

Annette's eyes welled up with tears. *My hard heart,* she reflected to herself. She soon learned from Lucky that the boy was in the same ICU that Joshua was in— possibly even the same bed. Annette invited him into the house, and made him some coffee and then called me to come home.

As I spoke with Lucky, we decided together that the church would do a funeral for his son. In the Balkans, survivors usually place an obituary with a picture in the newspaper. This cost about $30 and we provided the funds for it. Lucky went home and returned to the church the next day.

Calling together the leaders of the church, we met to plan out the funeral. Others also knew Lucky, and they came to assist in whatever way they could. We were gathered at the church building when Lucky came shuffling in to join us. He was despondent and very concerned. When queried about the problem he told us that the city was asking for $150 for a "pauper's plot" at the cemetery. We dipped into the church's funds and gave him the help he needed. He went to gather his family and friends, and we were to drive to the cemetery to meet there. This would be the first time we would ever hold a funeral as a congregation.

The biggest public cemetery in Sarajevo is called

The Lions. We arrived there and began looking for the plot. Unable to find it, we asked the gravediggers where Lucky's son would be buried. "Not here—not today, anyway," was the reply. Realizing our mistake, we quickly loaded up in the cars and headed off to Sarajevo's other large cemetery that is in the hills behind the Olympic stadium. Once again, there was no Lucky in sight.

One of the women from the church, a nurse, used a cell phone to call the State Hospital and inquire about Lucky's son. No child was admitted in the last week, nor had any child died. She tried the other major hospital and found the same to be true. We had been scammed.

There was no boy dying in an accident—only a con man and gullible Americans. It turns out that Lucky did have a son. Some of the church members had met him. He knew our church well enough to know that we wanted to help people. The only thing that saved me from serious embarrassment was the fact that it wasn't only the foreigners that had been taken. The Bosnians themselves thought that he was telling the truth.

I was furious. How could anybody be so crass as to steal on the lie of your own son's death? Were they so wicked that they would manipulate such a thing as this to their advantage? I wanted to leave this wicked country and go back to my own homeland to be safe from the sins of this black place. Annette was also angry. Lucky had played on her guilt. Her son, Joshua, survived. She had food, clothes, and an intact family. He had none of these and skillfully played her emotions to his financial advantage. She was vulnerable. Once the game began, he stuck with it until it paid off.

Why was this happening to us? Had we not prayed against this sort of evil attack? Joshua's recent brush with death, the weight of the work before us, the seemingly insurmountable obstacles all came together in a flood of anger and hurt. We were emotionally drained, and wanted to pack up and go home. I made a phone call to my field leader. Although he didn't know it, when I picked up the phone I had every intention to resign. As I explained to him what transpired, he gently reminded me that the progress we were seeing in the new church would not go unnoticed by the forces of evil. In retrospect, Annette and I agreed: It was a counter strike for the recent baptism service that was held.

Were they so wicked that they would manipulate such a thing as this to their advantage?

After some months of ministry there were a number of new believers who were asking about baptism. When the church started the work in Novi Travnik the war prevented any kind of a public baptism, so the first converts there were baptized in the bathtub of an apartment. In Sarajevo we were able to choose a more scenic venue for our first post-war baptism. In the western suburb of Ilidza is a stone bridge that dates back to the time of the Romans. It was one of a large network of roads that spanned across the Balkans enabling soldiers and traders to come and go between the western and eastern halves of the Roman Empire. The bridge, undoubtedly rebuilt many times over, still stands over the Bosna River.

We didn't really know how the authorities or the local residents would react to a baptism service, so we gathered early one Sunday morning to avoid a confrontation. Three trees lining the river waved in a slight breeze under the bright blue sky. The bridge reflected off the river as the baptism participants prepared. The river's source is not even a mile away from the bridge, bubbling out of the side of Mount Igman. The water is crystal clear and painfully cold. We agreed beforehand that there would be no sermonizing, only a few short scriptures and a homily.

A crowd of more than 100 people stood in a semicircle at the river's edge. A guitar appeared and some choruses were sung. I then walked out into the river as one of the other leaders called out the name of a person who would then walk out and turn to face the crowd. They were asked two questions: "Have you received Christ as your Lord and Savior?" and "Are you being baptized today of your own free will?" After whispering, or in some cases, shouting *"DA!"* ("YES!") they were lowered into the chilly water.

The spring water that was bubbling out of Mount Igman was so cold that as we baptized Mijlenko, he almost passed out and could hardly stand up again! As they walked out of the water the crowd sang a song of praise. Nineteen people were baptized that day. One of them was my son Caleb, which was a great thrill for Annette and me. (Our son Joshua would later be baptized in the same spot, along with two new Kosovar brothers.)

This was the kingdom expanding amid a city and nation where Satan had freely roamed. Mike was right: There was no doubt we had gotten the attention of not only heaven, but also hell. We saw professions of faith, baptisms, and gathering communities of believers. God was granting us favor.

Satan was not about to let that go on without a struggle.

— ❧ —

CHAPTER 8

MINISTRY
IS A
TEAM SPORT

"If you want to go fast, go alone.
If you want to go far, go together."
—AFRICAN PROVERB

In the weeks leading up to NATO's bombardment of Serbia in 1999 we found ourselves at a conference in Sofia, Bulgaria. Missionaries from all over Eastern Europe gathered for a time of teaching and fellowship. One of the highlights was hearing about the explosive growth of the Bulgarian church that had not evidenced much growth in years past.

At the close of the conference our family and three others decided together that we would take a shortcut through southern Serbia and back to Sarajevo. We decided that rather than driving alone, we would break up into two convoys of two vehicles each. It turned out to be a good decision.

Snow had fallen the night before. Some of the vehicles in the parking lot were not able to make the short hike uphill to the hotel's front doors. We packed chain and were not too concerned about weather as we crossed the border into Yugoslavia.

Making our way across southern Serbia we entered the mountains that cut through the entirety of the Balkans. Higher and higher we climbed, and as we did, the snow became thicker and wetter. Toward late afternoon things began to look downright icy, so we pulled into a gas station and I put tire chains on the front wheels of our van. I was sitting next to Art Arreguin in his four-wheel drive vehicle. In the seat behind me were my girls, Abigail and Sarah. Behind us in the blue minivan were Annette and Tammie Arreguin, the Esler boys, and the Arreguin children.

Art and I were busy talking about different things related to the ministry as we crested a large downhill slope. To our left and right there was a deep drop-off into fields below. By now it was dark, the snowfall was heavy, and the wind was blowing hard. As we began our descent Art's eyes grew large, and he said, "Ted, start praying, they just went over the edge."

"Yeah, right," I replied not realizing that this was no joke.

Art repeated, "I said start praying, the other van just went over the edge of the mountain!"

Art slowed down and looked for a place to pull over. We drove back up to the top of the hill but we couldn't see where our wives and kids went off. There was nothing to see since the drop-off was so steep.

Suddenly, Annette's head popped up over the roadside and she began calling for us as we rolled by with the windows down. "Everyone is OK," she yelled, "but we need your help passing the children up to the road."

As they crested the top of the hill, the back end of the van simply spun around in a circle and over they went. Sliding backward the van was airborne for a few seconds until it gently landed in the tall grass and snow and began hurtling downhill. About 50 yards down there were four

The back end of the van simply spun around in a circle and over they went.

trees growing up, forming a small nook into which the van slid. Small saplings further up the hill slowed the van before the impact. Two of the trees caught the back of the van and two caught the side. Some of the lower limbs punched out the windows and slightly grazed the head of the Arreguins' daughter, Larissa. It was miraculous that they weren't all killed in a roll-over.

Not knowing how secure the vehicle was, they slowly got out of the van. Art climbed down, and we carefully helped the children make their way out of the vehicle and up the incline onto the road. We couldn't stay at this spot because there was no place on the road. Walking up to Art's parked vehicle, we spotted a cleared area where we gathered together in nervous excitement to learn more of what happened.

As Annette and Tammie went over the edge they were talking. "This could be it," Annette said. Tammie recalled that she didn't feel afraid.

We were 11 people with one vehicle to get home. All Americans were told not to travel through Serbia, and we felt the need to hurry through on our way home. We were a little tense and wondered what we should do next. We gathered in a circle, held hands, and started praying. We gathered and prayed with thankfulness, and the children commented on how God preserved them. Their prayers were filled with praise and thanks. It was incredible time of fellowship that I am sure none of us will forget.

Art looked up from praying and asked, "What are we going to do?" The temperature was dropping, and it was getting very cold. Someone suggested that it was possible one of the other families on our team would be driving by. As we discussed whether or not this was possible, the Jones' Suburban crested over the mountaintop with the Prices' van right behind it. More then enough room for all of the kids and wives! They piled in and were soon heading toward home.

Art and I were left to get the van up from the steep incline. We called a tow truck who started by attaching a cable to the vehicle and pulling it up. His large tow truck promptly slid to the edge, almost teetered over the side, and finally settled down again. Now we had a real problem, and I began thinking, *We're not going to get this car out!*

As we talked to the tow-truck driver, he found out we were Americans. "We love Americans here, especially with ketchup!" he teased. He waved down a semi-trailer truck that was going by and asked the driver to park on the opposite side of the road. Anchoring to this semi-trailer he again applied power to the winch only to see both vehicles move toward the edge. Another truck was drafted, and the van slowly crawled up the side of the mountain and up onto the road. The whole process took more than five hours.

The van's windows were smashed out in the back and on one side. One of the tires was peeled off the van. Art and I put the spare tire on and decided to try to drive it home. We left at 1 a.m., after having driven the whole day previous, and we got into Sarajevo the next morning at 9:30 a.m. It was the coldest day on record in southern Serbia in 57 years. Since all the windows were smashed out, by the time we arrived, my body temperature was several degrees lower than normal.

When you live in a place like Bosnia, a team is more than a group of people with whom you work. They not only help you in difficult circumstances like these, but they also become your family. The first person from Pioneers to go into Sarajevo during the war paved the way for the team that would eventually live there.

A church leader from Croatia called Mike Johnson, then a Pioneers area leader, about a need for supplies to be distributed to Sarajevo. To make the trip in he would need to drive into the siege using the infamous Mount Igman Road. This is the route the United Nations used when the Serb forces were in a good mood.

Igman, located on the western edge of Sarajevo, is not a large mountain but had great importance for those living in Sarajevo. All traffic in and out of the city went down the narrow alley of death that was exposed to Serb gunners. The only other way into the city was by foot through an underground tunnel. Night signaled the start of a bizarre rush hour: Vehicles of all makes tempted fate and rushed down the narrow dirt strip toward the airport.

Reaching the crest of the mountain Mike could easily see the whole valley that cradled the city of Sarajevo. He was stopped by a Bosnian Army checkpoint and handed over his papers. The soldier on duty handed them back after a quick glance and Mike breathed a sigh of relief. He made it past the first and often most difficult test: proper paperwork.

Mike spent an hour talking with the Bosnian soldiers, telling jokes and sharing a cup of coffee with them. It was a snowy, cold outpost located in the woods. These men had obviously been there for some time, unshaven and rugged. As the sun began to set, more and more people gathered at the top of the mountain in preparation for the darkness that would hide their dash down the mountain. A column of tanks and armored personnel carriers suddenly appeared. It was a French battalion, and they were planning to go down the Igman Road as well. Mike asked the commanding officer if he could follow along behind this column of vehicles. The commanding officer agreed that he could, as long as Mike stayed toward the tail end.

Since the van Mike was driving was white, he hoped that in the twilight the Serbian gunners would mistake it for a U.N. vehicle. The commander of the column, however, was rather pessimistic that that would happen. "There's many a blown-up car and van scattered along the road," he said. He explained that the Serbs were strafing the road with 30 mm anti-aircraft rounds. If one of the shells hits a car, it basically explodes it and everything inside. There would be no survivors. Later, Mike would see that the commander was not lying. The side of the mountain was strewn with more than 100 vehicles that had simply been pushed over the edge of the mountain many with the bodies still inside.

As the column of tanks and armored personnel carriers headed out, Mike joined their ranks. The vehicles went down to the last safe spot where there was still a bit of cover. Once they rounded this curve, it was a couple miles down the mountain on a dangerously narrow dirt road. On the right was a drop of about 100 feet. On the left was the rock face of the mountain. The goal was to speed down as quickly as possible so that the Serbs couldn't place you in their crosshairs. Mike knew that his best chance was amid this column of French vehicles.

It was a horrendous drive. Tailgating a tank, driving at about 40 miles per hour down a totally dusty, curvy road, Mike could only see about 12 feet in front of the van. At the bottom of the hill the road turned sharply to the right through a French U.N. military battalion. Then he was at the bottom of the hill, safe at last.

One week after Mike's trip down Mount Igman, the U.S. Government had sent delegates to Sarajevo to begin work on the Dayton Peace Accord. Three Americans were killed on this very road, including one of the chief negotiators. What happened, it was reported, was that the armored personnel carrier simply drove off the road by accident and rolled over, killing everyone inside. Some of us suspected that it was actually hit by the Serb gunners but that explanation would have drawn unwanted accusations at a time when negotiations were the most delicate.

By this time the city was totally dark. One could not use headlights in the city for fear of the sniper's lone bullet. The western side of the city was already destroyed, and the war was raging that night. The only light was from artillery and mortar rounds that crashed into the buildings.

The tanks and armored personnel carriers that Mike was following turned off into their quarters, and Mike was left alone on the Sarajevo streets. Mike knew from the previous trips he made into the city that he was driving down Sniper Alley, but basically out of the immediate range of Serb guns.

The only place to spend the night was the Holiday Inn. The top third of the hotel was totally demolished on the inside. However, the bottom floors were still being used as a hotel. It was also one of the few places where you could get something to eat, though the prices were steep. As he drifted off to sleep that night the air was alive with the sounds of rifle fire and mortar shells.

The next day Mike met up with the remnant of the Baptist church. About fifteen people came to a worship service that Sunday. Every three to five minutes a crash from artillery or a mortar round was heard. "It certainly encourages prayer!" they joked as they fellowshipped together. Unfortunately, the war would take a toll on this small group of believers, leaving just a scattered handful by the time the shells stopped flying. It would be this group that I would later shepherd. Mike braved the bullets and shells to partner with this brave church.

Rob Farnsley, "Uncle Rob," as our kids know him, was the first person to officially join our team, which at the time was made up of Annette, the kids, and me, while we were living in Croatia. Rob was a realtor in California when he met Steve Richardson, who was then a missionary working in Indonesia. Steve challenged him to consider "leaving it all behind" and heading off to Indonesia, which Rob did a few months later. Eventually he found himself working in our agency's U.S. office and longing to go back to the "front lines." Little did he know that his wish would be granted—literally.

Rob's first foray to Bosnia happened when the war was at its height. There was fighting all over the country, and Sarajevo was already under siege for a couple of years. Once again, Mike was on a mission to deliver humanitarian aid. Mike had made a contact in a hospital located in the northern part of Bosnia, and he needed to verify the need before medical equipment could be sent.

Rob's first night in Bosnia was December 31, 1994, and he and Mike spent it in the city of Kiseljak in the U.N. complex. Machine guns were going off all around the compound in celebration of New Year's Eve and Rob huddled down in his bed, putting the covers over his head and praying that God would transport him to another place. It was incredibly loud.

That night they met a doctor in the small hospital in Gradacac. The doctors in wartime Bosnia were heroes. They worked long hours for no pay. That night the three of them gathered around a small light bulb and talked about the war, life, and what the doctor had been through. In the next days, Rob and Mike left with plans for Rob to return.

A shipment subsequently was arranged from a donor in the United States some months later. Rob traveled to Split, Croatia, and began his journey back into Gradacac. A driver and truck were hired, and they drove through Croatia on their way to central Bosnia.

When the shipment was leaving the cargo terminal a seal was placed on the door of the trailer. It was supposed to remain intact until the delivery was made. A customs official ran a wire through the outside latch and then pressed a lead weight on it, stamped with the date of entry. In this way, they could prove that there was no contraband added to the shipment as it traveled through Croatia.

Making their way to Mostar, Rob and the driver approached the border of the self-declared Croatian Republic. This was the first of a series of checkpoints one had to pass through on their way to the interior of Bosnia. A border guard motioned for Rob to get out of the truck and come to the back. He reached up and yanked off the seal, claiming that it was obviously not put on correctly and accusing him of not following the orders of the customs office.

Unfortunately, this was all part of a well-practiced scam, and Rob was its most recent victim. Rob pulled out a wad of cash and paid the "fine." It was deflating to be on a mission of mercy and be treated in this way.

The next morning they delivered their supplies to the hospital. The hospital staff was very grateful to get the items. Drinking coffee and talking about life with these people, Rob knew what he had to do. He began planning his move to Bosnia.

During this time, our team was involved with a number of humanitarian-aid projects. One of them was distributing some teddy bears that ladies in the United States made for the Bosnian children. They had written ahead and asked if they could include a tag on each teddy bear that would say, "Jesus loves you." Instead of the correct phrase, *"Isus te voli,"* they came with *"Isus ne voli."* This means, "Jesus doesn't love you!" We cut the tags off.

Rob traveled into Bosnia to deliver these and other items to needy people. During his travels, Rob met a gentleman whose name was Boris. Boris was from

Switzerland, but had grown up in Yugoslavia and knew the language of Bosnia. Boris asked Rob if he would be interested in going in and meeting his friends and family who lived in the central Bosnian town of Novi Travnik.

At that time, they were still shelling Novi Travnik. Rob moved to Mostar, and he was driving to Novi Travnik to get to know these people better. As Rob and Boris came into town bringing food and clothing, they would tell people that they were going to have a time to study the Bible. Mike visited and they held a number of evangelistic meetings. It was during these meetings that a family made a commitment to follow Christ. This was the first time that one of our team members experienced the joy of seeing new believers come to know Christ in Bosnia.

The Bible talks about finding a "man of peace" through whom the gospel can spread. In Novi Travnik, that person was Stevo. His apartment was often packed with people who wanted to hear the message of Christ. The first time that I visited Stevo's house, people continued knocking on the door throughout our Bible study, and they had to be turned away because there was no room for them. Within a few weeks, Rob held the first baptisms in Stevo's bathtub.

A few months later the Dayton Peace Accord was

signed. Two more families moved from Croatia to Bosnia. Sarajevo was still fairly dangerous but there were other cities that one could live in where there was no fighting in the immediate area. These families decided to move to Zenica. After Sarajevo, Zenica has more Muslims than any other city in Bosnia.

When they first moved in they were introduced to people from the fellowship that already existed in neighboring Novi Travnik. It was a similar situation in that the initial people that they met were interested in hearing about the gospel and within a very short time they also had a new church fellowship that was meeting regularly.

From all over the Balkans God's people were at work in significant ways. One woman, Blazenka, became a voice for the poor and oppressed in Sarajevo. It happened because she walked in their shoes.

During the early days of the fighting, many husbands made an attempt to get their families to safety. Little did they know that the siege of Sarajevo would last for as many cruel years as it did and that they were not going to be able to see them for a long time. One such family was the Dumic family. Mario was a Croatian but chose to stay behind to defend Sarajevo. Blazenka, his wife of Serbian descent, fled with their son to Croatia to be with his relatives. This was not to be. Bosnian Serbs were not finding much hospitality in Croatia due to the fighting between their newly formed nation and Serbia. Blazenka found herself in a box car, living as a refugee in northern Croatia.

A Baptist church in northern Croatia was reaching out to these refugees. From week to week they visited and helped to feed and clothe the people. They invited the refugees to help with the distribution. Life touching life, day after day led to months of close contact. Blazenka saw the love of Christ in the relationships between the church members. She surrendered her life to Christ. Not soon after a visitor arrived at her box car, Franklin Graham. She related her story to him and together they prayed for Sarajevo.

After learning the logistics of humanitarian-aid distribution, she became a leader in the effort to serve refugees. NATO moved into Bosnia, and Blazenka was not far behind. The first days that Blazenka was in our church I didn't quite know how to direct her. She had zeal and a passion to serve others, but the church didn't have the right structure or framework to fulfill her dream of a national-led humanitarian-aid effort. Soon, however, I learned that the church didn't need to help her: She was there to help the church.

Through the Croatians that served her, she began serving others. They sent her shipments of aid, and she registered her efforts with the local government officials. She diligently managed an aid outlet to desperate refugees. She never asked if they were Serbs or Croats or Muslims. She knew that the first time they entered her warehouse the most important question was, "Will they help me?" She was filled with sadness when she learned of their living conditions, conditions she and her son had endured. She smiled with them when they sheepishly accepted the assistance that was extended. She shrewdly knew when people were trying to take advantage of the free offerings. Through her loving care and attention to detail, many in the neighborhood in which she worked came to know that Jesus' people cared.

Her husband, Mario, was highly suspicious of Blazenka's new faith. It was the faith of such a small minority of people: How could it be true? He had risen to a position of influence in Sarajevo as one of the few Croatians who stayed to defend Sarajevo. For months he critiqued and studied the Scriptures. Blazenka asked us to pray. Mario began attending fellowship meetings. One day he accepted Christ. I must admit, as Mario has been quick to point out many times, my first reaction to this news was, "That's impossible!"

God plucked Blazenka out of a sea of refugees and called her to Himself. He then used her in mighty ways to overcome the hatred that prevailed in Bosnia. The greatest gift, though, was probably when her family was made whole in Christ. Blazenka was just one of many who were building Christ's church. The team was growing past the borders of the missionary band.

While working in Sarajevo we came into contact with a family from Konjic, a city to the southwest with 40,000 people. In that city we met a woman who was a refugee in Croatia. While she was there she met some Christians and became a believer. When she returned to her home, she began organizing humanitarian-aid distributions through the church in Croatia. She was a new believer, and there wasn't any spiritual aspect to her ministry. She got my name from the Croatians, and she called me and said, "Please come, we need to have a meeting." At this time I was so involved in other projects that I just couldn't do it and so I told her no. She called again and again. Finally I asked her, "If we had a meeting, how many people could she get together?"

"A hundred to 200 people," she answered. I thought she was exaggerating just to get us to come down. I told her to organize a meeting in a house and I'd come, bringing Gary Levi with me. He would share something with the group, and I would translate.

Arriving in Konjic, we found the house for the proposed meeting filled with so many people there was nowhere for us to sit. There were people standing outside the open windows listening. Levi started in Genesis 1, telling the story of creation. Within a very short time, we saw as many as 20 people profess faith.

One of the things that we learned from our experience in Konjic is that humanitarian aid can be a poor foundation for church planting. People who come to study the Bible in order to receive something like food or clothing are not those on which to build a congregation. Missionary work must be accompanied by good works. However, the objective is not to "make converts" or grow a congregation. It is to help people see the person and work of Christ. Ultimately, this little congregation suffered many problems as a result of greed. Many of the people were "Rice Christians," who were coming predominately because they were hoping to receive something. We determined that the best thing for us to do was to shut down the distribution of humanitarian aid and just concentrate on the Bible study and the spiritual aspect of the work. In doing so, it split this little group and it never quite recovered.

Some missionaries work for years in one place and never see the fruit of their efforts. Why were we being blessed so? No doubt part of the reason was due to our national colleagues from Croatia. About six months after we had moved to Sarajevo, the Croatian Baptist Union sent a young couple to work with us. One of the first projects they took on was the reconstruction of the old building that partially destroyed in Grbavica.

One misconception many have about the siege of Sarajevo is that the Serbs were only in the mountains surrounding the city. In fact, they occupied large sections of Sarajevo, including most of the suburb of Grbavica. One of the main features of this suburb is the Jewish cemetery located halfway up the southern hill, just a short walk from the river.

During the Spanish Inquisition the Catholic Church, which ruled Spain, ordered all Jews to leave the country. There was nowhere for them to go. Of all the cities in Europe, only Turkish Sarajevo would receive them. Most settled on this hill and had become merchants. Over the centuries they gave birth, lived, and buried their dead in Grbavica. Germany, with the assistance of the Croatian Nazis, rolled across Bosnia and swallowed up Sarajevo. The Jews were killed or sent to concentration camps in the north. Few Jews live in Sarajevo today. Other than this small remnant, only one temple and a graveyard are lasting reminders of their presence.

The graveyard is situated overlooking the city and affords a beautiful view. The crèche erected in its center is said to be the place where the first sniper fired on a protest march, killing a person and setting the stage for the most recent war. It would be on this hill that God would re-establish and grow our small church. It was to happen in the same building the Baptist church moved to some 80 years beforehand.

The nearby residents told us that in the early days of the war a jet strafed the entire area, dropping a bomb on the church building, which was really a large house. What was left of the upper floor was used as a sniper's nest. Small holes were cut in the cement walls through which a sniper could shoot. A fire had been set inside the building and destroyed some of the supports.

When we first began to pray about rebuilding this site into a church and outreach center, people scoffed at us. We only owned the bottom floor. As is common in Europe, a person may own part of a building. In this case, we had three rooms. Before we could do anything, of course, we had to find out if the building had land mines.

I called the local "Mine Awareness Committee" expecting them to dispatch a team to sweep our property. They got a nice laugh out of my request that they come over. What did they do? "Education only," was the answer. I spread the word that I needed some help with this, and a gentleman presented himself to me saying he would take the job for about $250. That seemed like a great deal, so we set a date and time.

Arriving at the property one sunny morning I pulled up in my little jeep and waited. A military vehicle came crawling up the road, and I thought, "Here he comes!" The troops waved at me as they drove by. Following them was a little red Zastava car. These small cars were made by the Russians and found all over Eastern Europe. A man popped out and strolled over to get his cash up front. I handed him the money and then watched him return to his car, where he carefully deposited the cash in the glove box. I was waiting to see what kind of land-mine clearing equipment he brought. Most of them use a hardened face shield with a metal detector and a prod. Often body armor is used as well.

Closing his car door he spun around and proceeded to walk every square inch of our property, stamping the ground and shaking the bushes. He even went into the building and checked out every room. As I watched, stunned, he exited the gate and told me, "Nope, no land mines." Not exactly the kind of equipment I expected!

A team from New Jersey came to clear the rubble out of the building. An estimated 40 tons of debris were removed, including hypodermic needles, guns, and Yugoslav Army Uniforms.

After the building was prepared, we lined up a lawyer and negotiated with the owner for the rest of the building and land. God provided the finances through a number of sources, and we were on our way. One donor, Hilfe Konkret's Director Johannes Neudeck, brought furnishings, materials, and even his own father to assist us in fixing up the building.

Our Croatian partners, as somebody from that part of the world, were much better equipped to lead the project. They dealt with teams of contractors, lawyers, city officials, and missionaries as they skillfully managed this project to completion. We called it "The Kairos Center." The Greek word *kairos* refers to "opportune time." It is similar to the thought captured by the phrase "window of opportunity." This center was opened for just such a moment in the city of Sarajevo.

It contained a meeting room for church services, a kitchen, an English language library, a room for up to a dozen people to sleep, and an upstairs balcony. Situated on a beautiful lot, it became a place where worshipers could gather. It was also a place of outreach. English language courses, meals, and other events were held here as a means to share God's love with the community.

When we first started this project, some were shocked that we would even try. "It will just be blown up again," a neighbor said. "Why not just raze it and start over?" said the leader of another organization. Through it all, our colleagues slogged away and saw it to its completion. Was it just a building? It probably appeared that way to those who visited. To us it was so much more because it was transformed by faith, relying on God as we worked together to see it completed.

God grew local leaders as we worked together. We noticed more initiative and understanding of the kingdom of God, but we also realized that our role was changing. The day was coming when Annette and I would need to step aside.

———— ❧ ————

CHAPTER 9

AN
IMPORTANT
LESSON

—•—

"To open up and become sensitive to God's own mission could also mean that we begin to recognize the strangers as messengers, sent to us with a particular message, and that, therefore, before we preach to them, we ought to listen to their stories." —GERHARD HOFFMAN

How would God teach me that evangelism is not simply a presentation or method of ministry but that He was able to speak for Himself? He sent Snahid and a situation about wood.

What circumstances had to be created for me to wrap my head and heart around the principle of loving people in order that they might see Jesus? Miljenko: his letter of introduction and discovery that Christ's love crosses borders.

What did it take for me to learn that God was able to overcome the obstacles to faith that Sarajevo presented? The faces and stories are too many to count. The lessons significant.

How much more amazing would it be for the church itself to discover these truths? I was doing my best to pass them on. Our national colleagues were preaching faithfully from the Word. Our team as a whole, now numbering about 25 and partnering with a number of other organizations, was teaching and building up believers in their faith.

Still, cultures have corporate sins. In the United States we suffer from materialism. In the Balkans the prevailing sin is division. The church in Sarajevo came a long way in overcoming this sin. Whether one was a Serb, a Croat, or came from a Muslim background, they were all one in Christ. In a city rife with division and hatred, there is little that could be considered more counterculture. It would be dishonest to say that this was easy. It was also a delicate balancing act because the division was not trite. There was real hurt, and we had to be very careful about maintaining unity.

One morning a visiting speaker greeted the congregation with *"Shalom, Sala'am aleykum, i mir,"* which is really just wishing peace on the congregation in three languages: Hebrew, Arabic, and Bosnian. Sala'am aleykum, the Arabic, is an emotionally charged phrase in Sarajevo. To use it is to confirm one's Islamic background. As soon as the words were said, the older women in the church began to cry. A hue and cry issued forth over the next few days and serious breaks in our fellowship emerged. "How," I pleaded with God, "will we ever break through this and see the church fully united in Christ?" I didn't realize how artificial our unity was. Surely the work of a missionary could not be finished while there was such deep hatred in the church.

Once again, God was about to bring the forces of His kingdom together to teach the church in a radical way that they should stand against hatred. Once again, war would be the instrument that would break through this stronghold. This time, it was the war in Kosovo.

In January of 1999, just days after our van accident, NATO began bombing Serbian military installations, as well as strategic roads and bridges. Tension in Bosnia grew as Yugoslav airplanes attempted to attack the NATO base in Tuzla. Within a few weeks the once-proud Serbian military was reduced to treaty signing, but before that point was reached, tens of thousands of refugees fled south to Macedonia and Albania. Several thousand Albanian Kosovars also made their way north and found themselves refugees in Bosnia—a nation already filled with refugees.

Just outside of Sarajevo, a refugee camp sprung up, and a number of our team members began ministering to this newest wave of refugees. Since the social services in Sarajevo and the surrounding area were already overwhelmed, it was natural for our church to also consider the needs that the Kosovars had for food and clothing. The Sarajevo church had already begun to lay the financial groundwork for this outreach. It was about this time that I learned just how deep centuries of bad history could run in the veins of a Sarajevan.

Mihal, one of the first followers of Jesus in our little fellowship, was an indispensable administrator. He could patiently wade through days of bureaucracy to get a crate of goods released from customs, walk a foreigner through the process of renting an apartment, or handle complex car registration and licensing issues. If ever I needed to visit while he was "on the job" it would be at some dismal government office where he would be waiting with a smile on his face. As Mihal and I drove to meet one of our team members who had just relocated to Sarajevo, I began to discuss plans for ministering to the Kosovars.

Mihal fell silent and stared straight ahead—not commenting or showing any interest in this new endeavor. Finally I asked him, "What do you think about this?"

"Ted-eh," he replied gravely, "These Albanians are the dirtiest, most lying people you could ever meet. Take it from me; they will not be interested in Jesus. They aren't worth our efforts, especially when we have so many needs already."

"But Jesus loves them," I countered.

"No," he looked at me sharply, "These people are pigs."

I could hardly believe what I was hearing. I was stunned. This man, who himself was living with his in-laws because his apartment was destroyed, had no compassion for the thousands living in shanties and U.N. housing. This man fellowshipped with refugees each week and worshiped with those who had warred on his own hometown. He experienced the forgiveness and love of Christ. How could he hold such hardness in his heart? I soon learned that the prejudice against

"No," he looked at me sharply, "These people are pigs."

the Albanian Kosovars was a staple of the local mentality. "These Albanians," I was told by my landlady, "are all rich. They have money stored in their mattresses, yet they live like dirty animals." Another told me: "You cannot trust them. They will stab you in the back at the first chance."

Fortunately, those in leadership in the church were not of this same mind. They worked hard for the Kosovars, providing food and helping in whatever way they could. A small humanitarian aid post grew up around the efforts of a handful of committed people—run and operated by the church, not the missionaries. In these early days of ministry to the refugees there was little spiritual fruit to show for these efforts. Good works, wrapped in Christ's love, were the core of this outreach, and it was important work.

Still, I could not shake the thought that if the new Christians in Sarajevo were not able to see that Christ can overcome these prejudices, what good was it that we made such forward progress in the ministry? If they were truly to become the overwhelming minority that God intended them to be, they needed to learn that even the most despised are loved by God. To love Him, they must also love them. This simple truth, which I thought was taught and grasped, was dashed by the reality of a deep-rooted hatred expressed by one member of our church, but held by many.

Words were empty. It was going to take more than words to shake this hatred. "God," our team prayed, "please shatter the spirit of division, and unite Your church against it."

While others were concentrating on these humanitarian-aid efforts, a couple of other team members adopted the Kosovar refugee camp. Joe Horning and his wife, Rhonda, had moved into the area after living in Albania and learning the language. Greg Murphy joined Joe on many visits to this dreary patch of mud where the U.N. had erected temporary structures. These ambassadors for Christ offered the Albanian Kosovars something others did not: friendship. They were soon explaining who Jesus is and what He did for them.

Unlike many Christians who timidly share their faith, Joe and Greg boldly proclaimed Christ. It wasn't long before two young men, brothers, began to seriously consider the gospel message. First, one brother committed his life to Christ and then, a few days later, the other did as well. Their last name was the Albanian word for "Teacher of Islam." Their father was, in fact, the local imam at the mosque in their hometown in Kosovo.

These young men were filled with Christ's love and

joy. They were earnestly studying the Scriptures and soaking in as much of the Bible as they could.

New believers are naive to the ways of "church." They haven't learned the unwritten rules that are present in every congregation. They speak without realizing the impact of their words in this strange new social group. So it was with two young Albanian Kosovar Christians in the spring of 1999, when they walked down the aisle to join us for their first-ever church service. They had obviously never been to a Baptist church before; they sat in the front row.

Some of the church members already met these new believers and warmly greeted them, but most didn't know who they were. As it became apparent that they were Kosovar Albanians, eyebrows raised and a few heads shook in disappointment that these Muslims would be present for our service.

A Bosnian church service is similar to those held around the world in hundreds of cultures. There is singing, prayer, a time of announcements, teaching, and fellowship. In our service we could take advantage of the smaller size and usually the pastor allowed for a time of prayer requests to be presented from the group. One by one people stood and talked about missing relatives, a lack of a job, and concern for an unsaved friend.

Then the younger Albanian brother stood up and turned to look at the little fellowship. The room went silent. All ears strained to hear, and most anticipated something controversial to come out of his mouth. They would not be disappointed.

"I love you, and I love Jesus" he said, with a huge smile on his face. He went on to recount the love he received from so many Christians. It surprised him so much. He was taught many things about Christians, but they didn't turn out to be true.

"I love Jesus so much; thank you for letting me love Jesus with you here today." As he sat down the room was silent. It wasn't the uncomfortable silence that happens when somebody says something inappropriate. It was the group recognizing the Holy Spirit's presence in this young man and the awestruck reverence for the holiness of the moment. In that moment, worldviews shattered.

Out of the corner of my eye I saw Mihal. I looked over at him and he was looking at me. He had a small grin on his face and he slowly shook his head back and forth. He mouthed the words "Praise God" and lifted his hands in a gesture of surrender. It wasn't a moment of "I told you so." It was Mihal's surrender to the over-powering God of love, and he was filled with a powerful wonder and awe of its strength.

The family that saw itself as the overwhelming minority was joined by a team who took on this challenge. The team that saw itself in the same way was now passing on this responsibility to the small, growing fellowship. In fact, this responsibility was already taken up by the church. The church was now a seed, planted among the citizens of Sarajevo, which germinated, pushed its way up through the dirt, and was growing to maturity. It was time to sow some seed elsewhere.

As we prayed together that Sunday morning, I realized that over and over again God crashed through the sin that was prevalent in Sarajevo to present Himself in radical ways. I was no more than a bystander, placed there to watch and wonder at how He accomplishes His will. When He performed these miracles He was calling on me to worship Him. And I did.

THE WORLD'S
WAR ZONES

—•—

"Be kind, for everyone you meet is fighting a great battle."
—PHILO OF ALEXANDRIA

After leaving Sarajevo in the fall of 1999, I have filled various leadership roles in PIONEERS, first in Canada and then in the United States. These new roles give me the opportunity to travel and observe what God is doing all around the globe. It's a front-row seat to incredible, miraculous outpourings of God's power among unreached peoples. We live in era in which more territory has been gained for Christ than at any other time in history. Whether my travels have been to seemingly peaceful places like India or Thailand, or into some of the world's war zones such as Bosnia, Iraq, Sudan, or Israel, I have observed overwhelming minorities: small groups of Christians, sent into hostile regions to carry the good news of Christ's love to people.

"Tonight I am sleeping in the world's most famous war zone." I wrote these words in my journal some time ago. As I lay down that night the crackle of an occasional gun spiked the stillness. There were no cars on the road in this city—a curfew was being enforced by U.S. soldiers. Electricity and water had only recently been restored. This I wrote from a hotel room in Baghdad, Iraq, not Sarajevo, in August of 2003. Saddam Hussein had just been captured, and the politics of the region were far from settled. Everywhere were signs of war and, in contrast, life. Life for a new and struggling movement of God's people not unlike that we saw in Sarajevo.

War provides an incredible contrast for love. I have wondered why people say, "Wars (and all the terrible things of the world) are what cause me to conclude that God does not exist." For me, war has cemented my understanding that man is evil. If not for God, what good could exist? As others have said, war is hell. Few things are better than hell at illuminating the truth of heaven. This is not to say that all who experience war are spiritually enriched. Many endure war only to spend their lives shaking their fist at God. Others become convinced that there is no good in the world and others reach even different conclusions. Seldom, however, can one experience war and not wrestle with the great questions of life.

People fighting for their lives have a simple worldview: survival. The bare essentials of daily existence become the most important things. Gone are dreams of greater material wealth, prestige, and other false gods. In its place is a quest for deliverance. War zones are places of great introspection as one is faced with life and death. It has been my greatest blessing and deepest wounding to talk with people who have been hunted by other people. In every story there is a spiritual dynamic at work, and many people express this honestly.

As a young missionary sent to Sarajevo, I didn't understand this. I saw what most of us see: a city divided, or a nation divided, or peoples divided. We see the politics or the irreconcilable history. Unfortunately, this only tells the story from the standpoint of the news report. Real "war stories" are about the people whose lives lay in the balance. They are about the mechanic, the college professor, the mother, and the building contractor. They are about individual lives swept up in immutable events. Each life is interacting with God and seeking to make sense from the "non-sense" that is war...and life.

I recently visited Sarajevo to find the same lovely hills and villages and, unfortunately, the same hard hearts. The work there is going slowly. While the outright hostilities were ended by NATO's guns, the attitudes and emotions of division has not passed away. But the seeds of the small church have certainly been planted. Like small acorns, these little congregations may grow to mighty oaks. More workers are still needed, and there is much to pray for. Perhaps God has a place for you in His master plan for Bosnia.

A war of eternal proportions is also raging among every unreached people group in the world. How and when will they have the opportunity to experience Christ's love and be transformed by trusting in Him? The challenge before young missionaries is simple: drive their streets, drink their coffee, meet the people, and above all, share your life with them. Even if you must dodge their bullets, God will present Himself to them. You are along for the ride. He is inviting you to capitalize on the moments He creates. He will overwhelm them, and He is not in the minority.

Tank shells were used as soccer goals by the neigborhood kids

Unloading humanitarian aid donated from Germany

A rainbow, God's symbol of promise, over Bosnian neighborhood

Dobrinja - shattered buildings reflecting shattered lives

The annual winter ritual of chopping wood

Baptism in the icy cold Bosna River

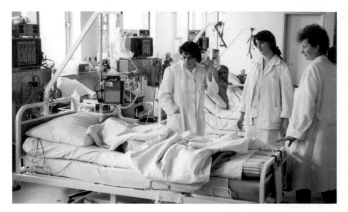

Joshua lies in the hospital after falling

U.S. troops mingle with neighborhood kids